THE SERMON ON
THE MOUNT

THE SERMON ON THE MOUNT

KINGDOM LIFE IN A FALLEN WORLD

Sinclair B. Ferguson

THE BANNER OF TRUTH TRUST

THE BANNER OF TRUTH TRUST
3 Murrayfield Road, Edinburgh EH12 6EL, UK
P.O. Box 621, Carlisle, PA 17013, USA

*

© Sinclair B. Ferguson 1987
Reprinted 1997
Reprinted 2006

ISBN-10: 0 85151 519 3
ISBN-13: 978 0 85151 519 9

*

Printed in the USA by
Versa Press, Inc.,
East Peoria, IL

Contents

	Preface	ix
1	The kingdom of God has come Matthew 4:23–5:2	1
2	What are you before God? Matthew 5:3–5	11
3	Filled with righteousness and mercy Matthew 5:6–7	25
4	Purity, peace and persecution Matthew 5:8–12	35
5	Future blessings now Matthew 5:1–12	43
6	The Christian in the world Matthew 5:13–16	55
7	Jesus, the law, and the Christian Matthew 5:17–20	67
8	The pure in heart Matthew 5:21–32	78
9	Oaths, eyes and enemies Matthew 5:33–48	94
10	Life with Father Matthew 6:1–8, 16–18	106
11	How to pray and live Matthew 6:9–15	118
12	Anxiety states cured Matthew 6:19–34	134

13	20/20 vision Matthew 7:1–12	148
14	Choices Matthew 7:13–29	160

To
Edmund and Betty Mitchell,
who first suggested this book,
and
Peggy, Alasdair, and Moira Brown,
and
in memory of Hugh

Preface

The Sermon on the Mount is probably the best-known part of the entire Bible. Some of its expressions have become part of our everyday speech. Even those who may never have heard of the sermon understand what we mean when we speak about 'doing unto others' or 'the salt of the earth'. Indeed, for some people, the sermon is 'the heart of the gospel,' and their whole philosophy of life is to 'live by the Sermon on the Mount.'

It is also the part of Jesus' teaching on which the most sermons have been preached and the most books have been written. Why, then, add to their number?

The answer is simple. The Sermon on the Mount speaks with extraordinary power and relevance to evangelical Christians today. In these pages I have tried to let it speak in a way that shows this power.

The sermon underscores something that marked the whole of Jesus' ministry. He stands before us as Saviour *and* Lord, Redeemer *and* Teacher. We can never divide Jesus in two, and take him in half measure. It is all or nothing. The 'forgiven' life and the 'holy' life are, in Jesus' view, two sides of the same coin.

It was once said of Jonathan Edwards, the famous American preacher, philosopher, and theologian (and instrument in great revivals), that 'his doctrine was all application, and his application was all doctrine.' Edwards must have learned that from Jesus, for that perfectly describes the character of his teaching in the sermon.

In our time we have lost that balance and mixture. We need to recover it, and recognise that in the kingdom of God, what we believe and how we live are joined together.

But there is another reason for writing on the sermon. It speaks to issues on which many of us have become fuzzy and confused. For example, what does it mean to have a Christian lifestyle in the pluralistic, secularised world in which we live? To what extent are Christians really 'different' from other people? How can we live like 'a city on a hill' that 'cannot be hidden' (*Matt. 5:14*)? Are our Christian faith and life as obvious to others as Jesus' words suggest they should be?

Jesus puts his finger on a number of issues of supreme importance: What is Christian character? What is the place of the law of God (if any) in the Christian's life? Is discipline important? How should we pray? How can we be free from anxiety in an anxiety-ridden world? What is so wrong about a judgmental spirit? Why do we need to have spiritual discernment? Is it possible for people to exercise 'spiritual gifts,' yet still not be true Christians? Jesus answers each of these questions in the course of his sermon.

Just to think about these issues is to realise how relevant the Sermon on the Mount is for us. As it was for those who first heard it, so it remains for us today, the *manifesto* of Jesus – his public declaration of his policy in the kingdom of God.

My aim in this study has been to expound Jesus'

teaching in a 'popular' way. After all, it was a 'popular' sermon when first preached (*Matt. 5:1, 7:28–29*)! I have avoided technical discussions and extended applications. These are valuable in their own place and time, but this book is intended to be what the French menus call an *hors d'oeuvre* – 'an extra dish served as a relish at the beginning of a meal.' My great hope is that, for individual readers, discipling relationships, and group study, and perhaps even families, this book will be precisely that, and give a new 'taste' for the teaching of Christ, and for a life of wholehearted obedience to him.

SINCLAIR B. FERGUSON
Westminster Theological Seminary
Philadelphia.

1
The Kingdom
of God
Has Come

MATTHEW 4

²³Jesus went throughout Galilee, teaching in their synagogues, preaching the good news of the kingdom, and healing every disease and sickness among the people.
²⁴News about him spread all over Syria, and people brought to him all who were ill with various diseases, those suffering severe pain, the demon-possessed, the epileptics and the paralytics, and he healed them.
²⁵Large crowds from Galilee, the Decapolis, Jerusalem, Judea and the region across the Jordan followed him.

MATTHEW 5

¹Now when he saw the crowds, he went up on a mountainside and sat down. His disciples came to him, and he began to teach them.

★　　★　　★

What is the Sermon on the Mount? It contains the

teaching of Jesus, but neither he nor Matthew calls these three famous chapters 'The Sermon on the Mount.' In fact, that title first came into use in the writings of the great North African theologian, Augustine of Hippo (354–430). He was quite right to call Matthew 5–7 a sermon, for here we have instruction and application rolled into one in a unique way. More than that, as in all sermons worthy of the name, there are divisions, there is development, and the message reaches a grand climax. *It makes a point!*

In studying any single text of Scripture, or an extended passage like this sermon, we should examine two things to help us understand it:

1. The general context in which it is set (in this case, the Gospel of Matthew).

2. The specific content in the teaching of the passage itself.

GENERAL CONTEXT

If you glance through Matthew's Gospel, you will notice that chapters 5–7 are part of a pattern that appears throughout the Gospel. Matthew 7:28 begins, 'When Jesus had finished saying these things.' That phrase reappears four times in the rest of the Gospel (*11:1, 13:53, 19:1, 26:1*), each time at the end of an extended discourse or block of teaching that Jesus had been giving to his disciples. In one way or another, these five sections all deal with the same theme: *the kingdom of God*. This was the great burden of Jesus' teaching.

Matthew had already introduced that theme when he summarised Jesus' ministry: 'Jesus went throughout Galilee, teaching in their synagogues, preaching the good news of the kingdom' (*Matt. 4:23*). His message was, 'Repent, for the kingdom of heaven is near' (*Matt. 4:17*). In a word, the message of the Sermon on the Mount is, 'This is what it means to repent and to belong to the kingdom of heaven.' The sermon is a description of the lifestyle of those who belong to that kingdom.

But what is the kingdom of heaven, and how has it come so near? From the way in which the expression *kingdom of heaven* is interchanged with *kingdom of God*, these two expressions appear to mean exactly the same thing (compare *Matt. 5:3* with *Lk. 6:20*). The kingdom is the rule or reign of God, the expression of his gracious sovereign will. To belong to the kingdom of God, then, is to belong to the people among whom the reign of God has already begun.

How can this be? Why is it that *Jesus* is able to say that the kingdom has already drawn near? Because Jesus himself is the King in God's kingdom. Where he reigns, *there* the kingdom of heaven is already present.

To those who first heard Jesus, this was a staggering message. They immediately understood (at least in part) what he was saying. He was claiming that the long-hoped-for day, the day of the reign of God, was no longer confined to the future – it was *now*. Jesus was preaching that the reign of God, promised by the Old Testament prophets (*e.g. Is. 52:7; Mic. 4:7*) had arrived! That explained the urgency of his call to repent. In the light of the presence of the King himself, a new lifestyle altogether was called for.

It is important to notice that the words '*from that time on*' act like headings for the main divisions of Matthew's Gospel. The phrase occurs for the first time in Matthew 4:17: '*From that time on* Jesus began to preach.' What was 'that time'? It was the imprisonment of John the Baptist (*Matt. 4:12*).

Later on, in Matthew 16:21, the same expression appears: '*From that time on* Jesus began to explain to his disciples that he must go to Jerusalem and suffer many

[3]

things at the hands of the elders, chief priests and teachers of the law, and that he must be killed and on the third day be raised to life.' Here Jesus explains more fully what kind of king he is to be. But what was 'that time'? It was Simon Peter's confession that Jesus was Christ, the Messiah, the King whom God had promised to send to save his people.

Matthew's Gospel, then, can be divided into three sections, punctuated by the expression '*from that time.*'

In the *first* section (*Matt. 1:1–4:16*) Jesus' identity is set before us, especially from the teaching of the Old Testament.

In the *second* section (*4:17–16:20*) Jesus is set before us as he fulfils the kingly authority of God's kingdom in his teaching, in his deeds of grace and power, and in his summons to enter the kingdom of God.

In the *third* and final section (*16:21–28:20*) Jesus appears as the suffering King who is crucified, but conquers death and sends his messengers out into the world to bring all nations into his kingdom. 'All authority in heaven and on earth' is his (*Matt. 28:18*). His is the kingdom and the power and the glory for ever!

In the context of the whole of Matthew's Gospel, then, we discover that the chief theme is *Jesus himself*. In each part of the Gospel we learn some new facet of Jesus' identity. The entire Gospel, and each part of it, centres on Jesus Christ – who he is, what he says, what he does. *The Sermon on the Mount should be understood in the light of this.* If we listen to it properly, with open ears and hearts, we will discover more and more about Jesus himself.

Why is that important? Because living out the Sermon on the Mount can never be divorced from a right relationship to Jesus Christ. That is what is so unique about this sermon. We can be helped through sermons given by preachers we do not know and may never meet. But that is not the case with this preacher or his sermon.

This teaching will change us only when we submit to the sovereign and gracious reign of the one who preaches it, for the Sermon on the Mount enshrines in its teaching the authority and lordship of Jesus himself.

Notice how this surfaces in Jesus' teaching. Being persecuted *for his sake* is one of the means through which God brings blessing on your life (*Matt. 5:11*). When Jesus expounds God's law (*5:21–48*), he is the interpreter to whom we are to listen: 'It was said,' . . . But I tell you' (*5:21–22; 27–28; 31–32; 33–34; 38–39; 43–44*). Whatever the precise meaning of these contrasts may be, they certainly underline Jesus' claim to absolute authority in interpreting and applying God's word.

Perhaps even more startling is the language of the climax to the sermon in 7:21–23. Here Jesus assumes the role of Judge of men. Every person's final destiny will be settled by whether Jesus 'knew' him or not (*7:23*). What is implied by Jesus here is stated explicitly in John 5:26–27: 'For as the Father has life in himself, so he has granted the Son to have life in himself. And he has given him authority to judge because he is the Son of Man.'

Nor was this claim simply a matter of words. Those who heard Jesus recognised a consistency between his person and his teaching. As they made their way home at the end of the sermon, it was his 'authority' (*7:29*) that formed the theme of their discussions.

Living the Sermon on the Mount means, fundamentally, bowing to the authority of Jesus. It means coming to him, taking his yoke, and learning from him (*Matt. 11:28–30*). This means that we must dispense with the myth (all too common) that we can have Christ as Saviour to begin the Christian life, and then at some later stage, make a full surrender to him as Lord.

That kind of thinking reveals a profound confusion about what the New Testament teaches. For one thing, we do not 'make' Jesus Saviour or Lord. We believe in him, trust him, receive him *as* Saviour and Lord. And further, if having Christ as our Saviour *means* belonging to the kingdom of God (as it certainly does), we cannot possibly live in his kingdom without his *being* King and Lord. In other words, if you are not seeking to live out the Sermon on the Mount, you lack the fundamental evidence that Jesus Christ is your Saviour, because the sermon is simply a description of the life of salvation.

But bowing to the authority of Jesus can be described more explicitly. He expresses his authority through his word, the Bible. It is, as John Calvin picturesquely put it, the sceptre by which King Jesus rules his people. It is *in Scripture* that Jesus continues to give us his teaching. When we read it, study it, and seek to obey it, we hear his voice and recognise his authority (*see Jn. 10:3–5*). That is why one mark of the Christian will be loving study of Scripture and a growing obedience to everything Christ teaches us through Scripture.

As you turn to the Sermon on the Mount, you ought to ask yourself if you have settled these issues in your own life. And you ought to pray that through hearing Christ's voice in the sermon, you will grow in settled obedience to whatever he says to you.

SPECIFIC CONTENT

The sermon, then, shows us the authority of Jesus. All students of Scripture recognise this. But *how* does the sermon reveal Jesus' authority?

All kinds of approaches to the sermon can be found in the church. Perhaps the most common one is to see it as a message calculated to produce the greatest possible guilt in the fewest possible chapters! It has often been presented that way: 'Here is the standard. Look how miserably you have failed. Pull yourself together and do better.'

This approach ignores what we have already seen is central to the sermon's message, namely, our relationship to Jesus Christ. To increase guilt is certainly not an evangelical interpretation of Jesus' teaching. But it has an evangelical variation that is also less than satisfactory. It is possible to see the sermon as a creator of hopelessness, driving its hearers only to despair. The sermon shows us what we ought to be as Christians, but fail to be.

We cannot avoid some sense of guilt as we read Jesus' words. Undoubtedly, as he describes the lifestyle that is appropriate to membership in his kingdom, we sense how far short of its glory we fall. But the sermon is not aiming to produce a sense of hopelessness and despair in us; rather, it is intended to set before us a glorious vision of what the Lord intends our lives to become. The sermon is Jesus' manifesto. It describes a regal lifestyle, the new behaviour pattern for the new kingdom we have entered.

A paradox lies at the heart of the kingdom. On the one hand it has already come near (*4:17,23*). It belongs to those who are poor in spirit and those who are persecuted because of righteousness (*5:3,10*). But in another sense, it is still to come. That is why Jesus teaches us to pray to God, 'Your kingdom come' (*6:10*).

How can the kingdom be here, and yet lie in the future? That may seem to be an abstruse, scholastic question, fit for discussion in the theologian's ivory tower, but irrelevant to life in the everyday world. Actually, it is one of the most practical questions any Christian could ask. It points us to the heart of the Christian life. It gives us a perspective that brings us to the secret of life in the kingdom of God.

The kingdom of God has come, in Jesus. Through faith

in him, we enter the kingdom. It belongs to us. But we live in 'the kingdom of the world' (*Rev. 11:15*), although we do not belong to it. We belong to a new order of things, a new age altogether, a new humanity in Christ. But that new life has to be lived out within the context of the old. The new lifestyle of the kingdom (the life described in the sermon) is to be expressed in a context in which it is opposed by the world, the flesh, and the devil (*1 Jn. 2:15–17*). This is why the battle in which the Christian finds himself is far fiercer than anything he knew before he became a Christian.

How mistaken we are when we think that, becoming Christians, everything becomes simpler, easier, less demanding. How could that be when we have entered a kingdom that is alien to the world in which we live and the life we used to have? If our King was tested, tempted, opposed, rejected, and eventually crucified by this world, should it take us by surprise that belonging to his kingdom involves us in a heroic struggle? Not only that, we have to fight a battle *within* as well! We carry into the new kingdom some of the habits and ways of thinking of the old kingdom. It can be a monumental struggle for us to be rid of them.

But we are sometimes told, perhaps by well-meaning Christian friends, 'If only you had the full measure of the Spirit, things would not be like that.' As a matter of fact, those who have a full experience of the Spirit are the very people who discover how fierce the conflict between the kingdom of God and the kingdom of the world really is. Those who live by the Spirit must *overcome* sinful desires; they are not immune to them (*Gal. 5:16–17*). Those who have the Spirit experience a fight to the death as they 'put to death the misdeeds of the body' (*Rom. 8:13*). Those who already enjoy the firstfruits of the final harvest of the ministry of the Spirit *groan inwardly* as they look forward to final redemption (*Rom. 8:23*).

This is why the Sermon on the Mount is full of *negatives*. Throughout his teaching, Jesus contrasts the way of the world (especially the religious world, but including the 'worldly' world as well) with the way of God's kingdom. We are often told not to be negative (notice the negative!). But that is bad counsel for those who would follow Christ. In his kingdom, being positive implies also being negative. Belonging to his kingdom means rejecting all the claims and the characteristics of this world's kingdoms. It means having a feeling of not belonging because you are 'strangers [aliens] in the world' (*1 Pet. 1:1*).

At the time of writing this book, I am an alien in the United States of America. To be very exact, I am alien resident number 37,669,045. There are millions of us, obviously! Sometimes I am asked about the differences between the United States and Scotland (my home country). I usually reply, half-humorously: 'Everything is different.' We use the same language, and many of us have the same ethnic roots. But many things about our lives – our accents, our currency, our electrical current, the side of the road on which we drive, the lines on our television screens, our sense of humour (and the way we spell *humour*!) – are quite different.

In a sense, almost everything is similar; yet everything is different. If only a few things were radically different, and these were easily identifiable, perhaps settling down as an alien resident would be relatively straightforward. But one of the struggles that every alien goes through is learning to live with 'the differences' while retaining his own personality and national identity. Many aliens, very naturally and understandably, fully identify with their new home. They become Americans, and may even accept the privilege of becoming citizens. But the more one struggles to retain one's national identity, the more conscious one is that one is an *alien* resident.

[9]

So it is with Christians as we live in this world. Our citizenship is in heaven (*Phil. 3:20*). This world is not our home. Its style of life is not ours. Yet we are not to live in a spiritual ghetto, apart from the world; in fact, we are its salt and light (*Matt. 5:13–16*). No wonder, then, if we find that the teaching of Jesus' sermon is as demanding as it is exhilarating!

The Sermon on the Mount teaches us about the lifestyle of the kingdom of God. That kingdom will be consummated only when Christ returns and transforms the kingdom of this world into his own kingdom, publicly putting everything under his authority. But the Sermon on the Mount is not about there and then; it is about here and now. It is not asking us whether we will live a Christlike life in heaven. It is calling us to lead that life on earth, as Jesus himself did to perfection. It is not a sermon about an ideal life in an ideal world, but about the kingdom life in a fallen world.

How do you react?

2
What Are You Before God?

MATTHEW 5

³*'Blessed are the poor in spirit,*
for theirs is the kingdom of heaven.
⁴*Blessed are those who mourn,*
for they will be comforted.
⁵*Blessed are the meek,*
for they will inherit the earth.'

★   ★   ★

When I was about seven years old, I was moved from one class at school into another. My abiding memory of that traumatic change in environment was listening to all the other boys and girls in my new class chanting in unison these words: 'Jesus opened his mouth and taught them, saying: "Blessed are the poor in spirit, for theirs is the kingdom of heaven."' My classmates had learned by heart what we usually call the Beatitudes. I did not know them, or where in the Bible they were to be found. And since I did not then know the Lord, it is not surprising that I had little idea what the words meant, even after I, too, had learned them by heart!

At first glance, the Beatitudes belong to a different world from the one in which we live. A beatitude is something we associate only with the Sermon on the Mount. We do not normally speak about people as being blessed. Even people who have been taught to speak of Mary, the mother of Jesus, as 'the blessed virgin' may not be clear about the meaning of the Beatitudes.

But the statements found in Matthew 5:3–12 should not have a foreign ring to those who are familiar with Scripture. The Book of Psalms, for example, opens with a beatitude: 'Blessed is the man who does not walk in the counsel of the wicked or stand in the way of sinners or sit in the seat of mockers' (*Ps. 1:1*). Similarly, Psalm 32 begins with two beatitudes: '*Blessed* is he whose transgressions are forgiven, whose sins are covered. *Blessed* is the man whose sin the Lord does not count against him and in whose spirit is no deceit' (*Ps. 32:1–2; Rom. 4:7–8*). The beatitude is clearly familiar language to the reader of the Old Testament. But what does it mean? Who is the 'blessed' man?

Blessing and its biblical opposite, *curse*, are words intimately related to God's covenant with his people. According to the Lord's promise and commitment, those who were faithful to him would experience his blessing on their lives. Those who turned from him would experience his curse and judgment. God's covenant with Abram illustrates this. When God called Abram, he promised to bless him, to make him a blessing to others, to bless those who blessed him, and to bring blessing to the whole earth through him (*Gen. 12:2–3*).

Later, in the covenant at Sinai, this is spelled out yet more clearly. Deuteronomy 28:1–14 contains all of God's promises to bless his people in their obedience to his covenant word, while verses 15–68 record the curses and judgment that would follow their disobedience.

This blessing is simply fellowship with God, the experience of his covenant promise: 'I will be your God and you will be my people.' It means having a right relationship to God, and enjoying him as we should. That is why the opening chapters of the Bible speak of God giving his blessing to his creation and his creatures (*Gen. 2:3*). Occasionally, the word *blessed* has been translated as *divinely happy*.

The Beatitudes, then, do not focus on what *we* are to do. Rather, they describe the blessings – the covenant grace and joy – that belong to those whose lives show the marks of the kingdom of God. In giving each beatitude in Matthew 5, Jesus also explains the reason for each blessing.

Sometimes we become a little confused about the nature of Jesus' teaching, and nowhere more commonly than in the Beatitudes. Jesus' words were not the expression of 'on-the-spot inspiration' or flashes of sudden revelation. Often his teaching took the form of exposition or application and elucidation of Scripture.

That is so in the case of the Beatitudes. In particular, Jesus was taking some of the themes of Psalms and Isaiah, and applying them to his disciples. He was pointing out what God's word tells us is the blessed life. The 'new' element was not that he spoke the Beatitudes. It was that he spoke against a background in which God's word had become clouded. People had lost sight of where true blessing was to be found.

Jesus' voice needs to be heard again, *by Christians*. How far we stray from his view of things!

That statement can readily be put to the test. What is your heart set on as vital for your life and your character? What eight things do you most want to see developed in your life? Perhaps it would be a good idea for you to make a list. Does it compare favourably with what Jesus says? Does the list include poverty of spirit, meekness, a hunger and thirst for righteousness, mercy, purity of heart, a peacemaking spirit, and a willingness to be persecuted for the sake of Jesus? Or do you think that real blessing is really to be found elsewhere?

Our Lord says that all other supposed blessings are mirages in the desert. They may promise much; they can supply nothing but disappointment. The only life that God blesses is the one marked by his values. They are the hallmarks of those who belong to the kingdom of God.

Christians vary greatly in every conceivable way, including personality, interests, social background and intellectual abilities. How different from one another we are! And yet, according to the New Testament, we all belong to the same family and have the same basic family likenesses. They are listed in the Beatitudes.

How often I have been both surprised and delighted to meet Christians I admire and respect for their service and ministry – men and women in most respects quite different from one another – whose personalities never-theless express these same basic hallmarks of Christ's family. This is possible because the same Christ trans-forms his people into his own likeness without abolishing their individual identities. That is blessedness in abund-ance!

The first three beatitudes describe the Christian as one who is poor in spirit, mourns, and is meek. There is a common element in these characteristics. It is the recogni-tion that what we are in the presence of God is what we are; no more, no less. Only such belong to the kingdom of God and receive the encouragement and comfort of his grace. Only such have their mourning turned into dancing (*Ps. 30:11*), and enter into the reality of the promise of the land given to Abraham (which was a picture of Christ and his authority over all lands).

Poverty of spirit is neither a financial nor a depressive condition, although it has often been mistaken for both. Some Christians have given away all their possessions on the basis of this beatitude, but a man can possess nothing and still lack this spirit. Neither is poverty of spirit a bad self-image, in which low self-esteem, introversion and morbidity predominate. Again, a man can be marked by all of these characteristics and yet know nothing of what Jesus meant.

In the Old Testament *the poor* is almost a technical term for a particular group of people. Psalm 34:6 speaks about 'this poor man' who called on the Lord and was heard and saved. In Psalm 40:17, the author describes himself as 'poor and needy,' and asks the Lord to remember him and deliver him. Similar statements elsewhere underline the fact that to be poor is to be weak and helpless, to be dispossessed and to lack the resources to defend and save oneself. The poor are the needy and the captives who 'seek God' as their only refuge and salvation (*Ps. 69:32–33*). They are the bankrupt of this world, who know themselves to be so, and who therefore trust in the Lord as their only hope of protection and deliverance.

But what is poverty of spirit? By speaking of the poor 'in spirit,' Jesus underlines the fact that he is not speaking about a lack of material prosperity. That may lead to poverty in spirit, but it is not identical to it. Indeed, physical poverty may harden our pride. Jesus is describing the person who sees his spiritual bondage, is conscious of the debt of his sins (*cf. Matt. 6:12*), and knows that in himself he is dispossessed before God. All he can do is cry for mercy, and depend upon the Lord.

No one can be a Christian without this spirit. Everyone who is a Christian has this spirit. It is the spirit of the prodigal son. He left his father proudly, self-assured in his share of the inheritance. But when he was bankrupt, 'he came to his senses' (*Lk. 15:17*). In humility of spirit, emptied of all his pride, he came home to his father, empty-handed, no longer full of himself but looking only for whatever his father might be pleased to give him. So it is with the Christian:

> *Nothing in my hand I bring,*
> *Simply to Thy Cross I cling;*
> *Naked, come to Thee for dress;*
> *Helpless, look to Thee for grace;*
> *Foul, I to the fountain fly;*
> *Wash me, Saviour, or I die.*
> A.M. Toplady

In the early chapters of Romans, Paul hints at how this new spirit is born. We discover that instead of being self-sufficient and acceptable before God, we are by nature rebels against him. We have broken his commandments. All that we have done on the assumption that it will earn favour with him simply disqualifies us from his presence. We are guilty all the way from the tongue in our head, which practises deceit, to our feet, which do not know the way of peace, and whose ways are marked by ruin and misery (*Rom. 3:13–17*). 'There is no one righteous, not even one; there is no one who understands, no one who seeks God. All have turned away, they have together become worthless; there is no one who does good, not even one' (*Rom. 3:10–12*).

What is the result of taking this divine indictment seriously, and applying it to ourselves as we think of the judgment seat of God and his verdict on our lives'? Paul does not leave it to our imagination: every mouth will be shut and silenced, and the whole world – ourselves included – will be condemned as guilty before God (*Rom. 3:19*). We who have boasted of our sufficiency, or our achievements; we who have thanked God that we are not like other sinners, will have absolutely nothing to say to our Judge. We will stand before him ashamed, silent, and utterly lost.

When God leads us to see that this is our real condition before him, and we recognise this to be so, then poverty of spirit is born in our hearts. Undeceived at last, we see that our only hope is in the Lord. We are poor men and women in ourselves, with no righteousness of our own to plead before God. We are bankrupt, debtors in his court. Our plea must be for mercy.

We are urged today to develop almost every other kind of spirit except poverty of spirit. But the lack of this spirit can lead to spiritual ruin, as Jesus warned the Laodicean church: 'You say, "I am rich; I have acquired wealth and do not need a thing." But you do not realise that you are wretched, pitiful, poor, blind and naked' (*Rev. 3:17*). We are in danger of being spewed out of Christ's mouth as if we were neither hot nor cold. There is much teaching on how to be filled with the Spirit, but where can we learn what it means to be spiritually emptied – emptied of self-confidence, self-importance, and self-righteousness?

The sad truth is that we know so little of the blessing of which Christ speaks (and which he gives) because we are all too often full of ourselves and our own means of blessing. In fact, there is no sadder commentary on our lack of this spiritual poverty than the readiness so many of us have to let others know what we think. But the man who is poor in spirit is the man who has been silenced by God, and seeks only to speak what he has learned in humility from him.

[17]

If you would be rich and possess a kingdom, you must first lose all – including yourself and your self-centredness – and become poor in spirit.

MOURNERS WHO ARE COMFORTED

Mourning is grief and sorrow caused by profound loss. We usually associate it – and the beatitude that those who mourn will be comforted – with death. But that kind of mourning is in fact the most painful form of a widespread experience. What we feel when we are deeply disappointed in a friendship, or lose our job, or fail an exam, are also forms of mourning.

Is Jesus, then, giving us a word of general encouragement in what he says here, assuring us that sorrow will eventually abate? Is he saying, 'Keep going. It will soon pass. Time heals all wounds'? That would be far too superficial a reading of the Sermon on the Mount.

Jesus is speaking about life in the kingdom of God. The poverty he describes is in a man's spirit, not his pocket. Similarly, the grief Jesus describes is man's mourning over his own sinfulness; it is regret that he has proved a disappointment to the Lord. Numbed by the discovery of his poverty of spirit, he learns to grieve because of it.

Here, then, is another characteristic of the Christian. He does not excuse his sin, or belittle it, or ignore it. He does not weigh it in the balance with what he regards as his better qualities, or the fruitfulness of his service. Rather, he cries out with Paul, 'What a wretched man I am! Who will rescue me from this body of death?' Then he is comforted by the answer: 'Thanks be to God – through Jesus Christ our Lord' there is deliverance and comfort (*Rom. 7:24–25*).

As with all spiritual graces, it is possible for us to be deceived about the real nature of this mourning. It is emphatically *not* to be equated with a heavy and depressive spirit. Some of us by nature are melancholic, and sink more easily in our spirits. We become introverted and develop a poor image of ourselves that surfaces in the way we look at or address others, even in the way we hold our heads and walk. But all of these things can be characteristics of a person who is absorbed in himself; rather than is poor in spirit.

By contrast, the man who genuinely mourns because of his sin has been drawn out of himself to see God in his holiness and grace. It is this – his sight of God – that has made him mourn. Paradoxically, it is the same sight of God that will bring him comfort. The God against whom he has sinned is one who forgives sinners!

There is a classic example of this in Psalm 130. The psalmist is overwhelmed by his sense of sin. He sees himself before the judgment seat of God and confesses, 'If you, O Lord, kept a record of sins, O Lord, who could stand?' (*verse 3*). It is not just the fear of being discovered that overwhelms him. It is the knowledge that he has offended the Lord that fills him with shame and grief.

Yet, in seeing himself in the presence of God, the psalmist has also learned the astonishing fact that with God there is forgiveness; therefore, he is to be feared (*Ps. 130:4*). The sinner hates his sin, and grieves over it because it is an offence against God. But he mourns over it all the more because this same God forgives sin!

Some Christians never seem to discover this reality of life in God's kingdom. It is *grace* that makes us mourn for our sinfulness. The law of God convicts us of our sin (as it did Paul; see *Rom. 7:7–12*). But it is the grace of God that melts our hearts and causes a right attitude toward that sin, in sorrow, shame, and mourning.

Is this not a gloomy picture of what it means to be a Christian? Admittedly it is a contrast – and perhaps an antidote – to the contemporary notion that being a

Christian means being on a constant emotional 'high.' But is it true to say that the Christian constantly lives in a state of mourning, always crying out, 'What a wretched man I am' (*Rom. 7:24*)?

Three things should be emphasised here. The first is that whenever the Christian is conscious of his own sin, he will be grieved by it. Otherwise he will grieve the Holy Spirit (*Eph. 4:30*). But the conscious and psychological depth of that grief may vary greatly. Sensitivity to sin does not necessarily mean that a Christian is constantly in a state of despair.

The second thing to remember is that no single beatitude should be isolated from the others. Jesus is describing the whole Christian life in this sermon. We should not truncate his teaching by isolating one of its principles from the others.

Furthermore, a rounded spiritual experience involves stretching our emotional response to the gospel, not narrowing it. The child of the kingdom knows higher joys as well as deeper sorrows, more sensitive mourning but also more profound comfort, now that he is the Lord's. His emotional sensitivity becomes greater – *not less*.

Think of Paul in this connection. Do you not get the impression from the New Testament that when he was brought into the kingdom of God, he was changed from a shrivelled-up young man – knotted-up emotionally, spiritually, and psychologically, and living within a very confined range of human emotions – to a man whose emotional range from the heights to the depths was stretched to the limit? In some measure, that is true of us all. Being spiritually stretched involves pain – the pain of discovering the effects of our sin, the shame and grief of knowing how twisted we have been. That is the first stage in discovering the comfort of the gospel.

Jesus saw this as the fulfilment of Isaiah's promise about
the ministry of the coming Messiah:

> *The Spirit of the Sovereign Lord is on me, . . .*
> *He has sent me to bind up the brokenhearted,*
>   *. . . to comfort all who mourn,*
>   *and provide for those who grieve in Zion –*
> *to bestow on them a crown of beauty*
>   *instead of ashes,*
> *the oil of gladness*
>   *instead of mourning,*
> *and a garment of praise*
> *instead of a spirit of despair.*(Is. 61:1–3;
>   cf. Lk. 4:16–21)

THE MEEK WHO INHERIT THE EARTH

Poverty of spirit and mourning over sin have a pervasive
influence on our lives. Their immediate effect is to make
us *meek*.

The word *meekness* is notoriously difficult to define. It is
certainly not a lack of backbone. Rather, it is the humble
strength that belongs to the man who has learned to
submit to difficulties (difficult experiences and difficult
people), knowing that in everything God is working for
his good. The meek man is the one who has stood before
God's judgment and abdicated all his supposed 'rights'.
He has learned, in gratitude for God's grace, to submit
himself to the Lord and to be gentle with sinners.

Scripture provides two special illustrations of meekness. Moses is the first. He was the meekest man of his day
(*Numb. 12:3*). But the story of his life teaches us that *this
was not his natural disposition*. It was a quality that God
wrought in him over many years and with great patience.

In earlier days Moses may have been self-sufficient, and
like so many self-sufficient men, impetuous and self-
willed. Acts 7:25 seems to indicate that Moses had a sense

that God was calling him to lead the Israelites out of their bondage in Egypt. When he slew an Egyptian who was mistreating an Israelite, he 'thought that his own people would realise that God was using him to rescue them' (*Acts 7:24*).

It took forty years in the loneliness and isolation of the desert – forty years of tending sheep rather than shepherding Israel – before Moses' natural spirit was subdued by God, and he was prepared for the call he received from within the burning bush (*Ex. 3:1ff*). Those must have been years of testing for Moses; he may have despaired that he would ever be useful in God's service. Forty years as a shepherd gave him plenty of time to reflect on his sin, to mourn over it, and to learn patience and submission to the will of God.

This 'kingdom characteristic' of meekness is the clue to so much that God does in our lives, yet we too rarely recognise it. He wants us to be meek. But first he may have to break our pride, destroy our sense of self-sufficiency and humble us under his mighty hand before he uses us for his glory. He sends trials, reveals the secret ambitions we have hidden in our hearts, and uncovers our reliance upon ourselves. Then, as he patiently changes us, he develops within us this meekness of character. Now he will use us for his glory and for blessing others' lives.

The second example of meekness in Scripture is that of the Lord Jesus Christ. He is 'meek and lowly in heart' (*Matt. 11:29, A.V.*). In fact, this meekness is virtually the only personal quality about himself to which Jesus drew specific attention. He is indeed, in the biblical sense, 'gentle Jesus, meek and mild.' If we despise these words (written by Charles Wesley), we are in danger of despising Jesus' description of himself. Not only that, but we fail to understand what God intends to make of our lives too.

Meekness is especially important for those who are

servants of Jesus Christ. Isaiah thus describes Jesus as the Servant of God: 'He will not shout or cry out, or raise his voice in the streets.' (He does not draw attention to himself.) 'A bruised reed he will not break, and a smouldering wick he will not snuff out' (*Is. 42:2–3*). All the servants of Jesus are called to share these same qualities.

This is why, when faced with a congregation for which we might think 'a show of strength' would have been appropriate, the apostle Paul appealed to the Corinthians 'by the meekness and gentleness of Christ' (*2 Cor. 10:1*). For the same reason, Paul emphasised to Timothy that the Lord's servant should pursue meekness and gentleness (*1 Tim. 6:11*). The servant's instruction must be gentle, he must not be quarrelsome (*2 Tim. 2:24–25*).

There is probably no more beautiful quality in a Christian than meekness. It enhances manliness; it adorns femininity. It is a jewel polished by grace. But it is all too rare. Is that because so few of us know what it is to be poor in spirit and to mourn for our sins?

Poverty of spirit, mourning for sin, spiritual meekness – all these hallmarks of kingdom life can be imitated. We can counterfeit them. But just as a stone hurled into the air seems to defy the law of gravity, only to rise ever more slowly until it turns and plummets to the ground with increasing velocity, so it is with all cheap imitations of God's grace. They 'burn out' as they return to the atmosphere of this world. They cannot sustain themselves in a fallen world. Only the real thing will survive.

But how do these hallmarks appear in our lives? Our chapter began with the biblical answer to that question. Only as we come to know God and his presence do we begin to discover ourselves as we really are. When we know what we are before God, and look to him for grace and salvation, then we become poor in spirit; then we

[23]

mourn for our sins; then, having seen ourselves as we really are, we bow to his will in all things. And as we experience the gentleness of his grace, we are meek and gentle with others.

3
Filled with Righteousness and Mercy

MATTHEW 5

⁶*'Blessed are those who hunger and
thirst for righteousness,
for they will be filled.
⁷Blessed are the merciful,
for they will be shown mercy.'*

★　　★　　★

We have two basic spiritual needs. The first it to come to
understand ourselves, to discover what we really are in the
presence of God. His word reveals this:

*Sharper than any double-edged sword, it penetrates
even to dividing soul and spirit, joints and marrow; it
judges the thoughts and attitudes of the heart. Nothing
in all creation is hidden from God's sight. Everything is
uncovered and laid bare before the eyes of him to whom
we must give account.* (Heb. 4:12–13)

When God's word is expounded in the power of the

Spirit, we are forced, under its influence, to see ourselves in all our sinfulness. Thus, discovering ourselves, we become poor in spirit, mourn for our sins, and become meek before God. This is what Jesus has taught us already in his words of blessing.

But we have a further spiritual need. Driven *into* ourselves, we now need to be driven *out of* ourselves. Martin Luther said that man's basic problem was that he was 'incurvatus in se' – turned in upon himself, or self-centred. The work of God in giving us true knowledge of ourselves is not intended to increase this. Rather, it is the way to decrease it. For once we have discovered that we have no resources to save ourselves, we learn to look elsewhere – to Christ – to meet our needs, and also to meet the needs of the world in which we live.

The fourth and fifth beatitudes tell us that those who hunger and thirst for righteousness will be filled, and those who are merciful will receive mercy. These two beatitudes have a crucial significance in the spectrum of graces Jesus describes. They underline the fact that while we must discover the depths of our need, God does not intend that our lives should be paralysed by our sense of need. Instead he intends that we should be turned away from ourselves to his righteousness, and finding his righteousness, we should be turned toward others in their need of mercy.

This change from a heart dominated by and absorbed with itself, to a heart that reaches out for God and to others marks the turning point from immaturity to maturity in spiritual experience. In physical life the difference between childhood and adulthood is the transition from self-orientation to a recognition of one's place in the world. So in spiritual life the mature Christian is one whose life is centred on God and his will, and who seeks to serve others by God's grace.

[26]

HUNGRY AND THIRSTY

Hunger and thirst are fundamental physical needs. That was all the more true in Jesus' day in Palestine, where water was at a premium and food was sometimes scarce. For that reason, he uses these words to depict the intensity of the Christian as he longs for *the righteousness of God*.

The idea of righteousness occurs with some regularity in this sermon. It is one of the major themes: Christians may sometimes be persecuted because of righteousness (*5:10*); they must have a righteousness that exceeds the righteousness of the scribes and Pharisees (*5:20*); they do acts of righteousness (*6:1*); above all, they are to seek God's kingdom and his righteousness, in the assurance that everything they need will be supplied (*6:33*). But what *is* the righteousness of God?

The idea behind the biblical word *righteousness* is probably 'conformity to a norm.' Given that norm, righteousness is the situation in which things are what they ought to be. In the Old Testament, righteousness is associated with God's covenant. He is faithful to it. In relation to his promise, God always does what he ought to do, namely, fulfil his promise. That is why his righteousness can be expressed in judgment, or in salvation.

Often we associate the righteousness of God only with condemnation. But Scripture does not limit righteousness to this. It tell us that 'the fruit of righteousness will be peace' (*Is. 32:17*) and explains in Isaiah 45:21 what this means by telling us that God is 'a righteous God *and* a Saviour' (not, '*but* a Saviour').

To hunger and thirst for righteousness is, therefore, multifaceted. It means, first of all, to long for a right relationship with God, and consequently to be righteous before him. But it also means to desire to live rightly before him in the world, and to desire to see right

[27]

relationships restored in the lives of others. In a fallen world, to hunger and thirst will be continual in the Christian's life.

The righteousness we seek (our relationship to God being what it ought to be) has three dimensions. First, it is provided for us by Jesus himself. We have sinned, but God made Christ to become sin for us, so that in him (through faith) we might receive righteousness (*2 Cor. 5:21*). This is the centre of the gospel. We lack righteousness, but God provides it for us.

This was the discovery that changed the life of Martin Luther. In studying Romans, he wrestled with Paul's statement that the righteousness of God is revealed in the gospel. To Luther, this suggested that Christ stood before him as a hostile judge. In fact, in Luther's Latin version of the Bible, the word *righteousness* was translated 'justitia' (justice). The thought of Christ terrified him.

But then Luther began to discover what Paul really meant. He realised that Paul was not describing Christ as a judge but as a Saviour. The right relationship with God of which Paul wrote was offered by Christ as a gift. From that moment on, Luther called Paul's words 'the gate to Paradise itself!' He had hungered and thirsted, indeed, for righteousness, and God had satisfied him!

But this is only one dimension of the righteousness of God for which we are to long. It has a second aspect. We cannot welcome Christ as our Saviour (as Luther did) without being willing for him to be precisely that – *Saviour*. As such, he saves us from sin's power and its influence. He not only brings pardon, but he works in us to make us live in our right relationship with God. Thus, in Romans 5:21, Paul says that God's grace reigns in our lives *through* righteousness. It is not only a gift! It is our reigning king in Jesus Christ. It reigns, and it does so through righteousness, never apart from righteousness.

Right living is what we hunger and thirst for, as well as forgiveness. If we do not, then our supposed longing for a right relationship with God is proved false. We cannot take Christ's gift (forgiveness), but neglect his demands (right living). It is one of the great tragedies of the church today that we have come to believe in what Dietrich Bonhoeffer called 'cheap grace' – a Saviour who leaves us much as we were, instead of actually saving us from sin.

Sometimes this distinction has been justified by speaking of 'carnal' Christians and 'spiritual' Christians, as Paul seems to do in 1 Corinthians 3:1–4. But Paul's point is that those whose lives do not exhibit practical righteousness are not just behaving like 'inferior' Christians; *they are behaving like people who are not Christians at all.* They are contradicting God's saving righteousness.

The third aspect of God's righteousness for which we long involves our seeking to see it established everywhere. We are to enjoy a right relationship with God. In our own lives, we are to live with moral integrity. In our dealings with others, we are to develop right relationships. In the world in which we live, we are to encourage moral integrity and right relationships, both by the work of evangelism, and by all we do to reform society and bring it into conformity to Christ's teaching. The work of evangelism and missions and the task of social reformation are not to be thought of as alternatives for the Christian. They go together. Each is an application of our desire to see righteousness prevail in God's world. That is what we mean when we pray, 'Your will be done on earth as it is in heaven' (*Matt. 6:10*)!

More than anything else, righteousness involves *right relationships* – between ourselves and God, between ourselves and others, and in the world at large. That is why the quest for righteousness can never be a hard-nosed pursuit. It is born out of a sense of personal need, and expands because of our sense of the world's need. The longing for righteousness issues from a broken heart. For this reason, hungering and thirsting for it is coupled with another beatitude that directs us to the caring quality of the true Christian.

GIVING AND RECEIVING MERCY

Jesus says that the merciful are blessed because they will receive mercy.

This presents us with something of a problem. Does Jesus mean that we will receive mercy only if we ourselves are merciful? Certainly that is his meaning. But this does not imply that the *cause* of our receiving mercy will be the fact that we were merciful, as though we had earned God's mercy. Being merciful is the natural result of receiving Christ and experiencing the grace of God. If we are not merciful, we cannot have received Christ's mercy, and therefore cannot look forward to receiving his mercy in the last judgment.

There is really no problem in what Jesus says about mercy. This manner of speaking occurs *later* in his teaching: Those who forgive the sins of others will be forgiven (*Matt. 6:15*). This does not mean that we merit forgiveness by forgiving others, but rather, that unless we forgive others, there is no evidence that we ourselves have been forgiven.

A similar point is made in the parable about the unmerciful servant (*Matt. 18:21–35*). A merciful person cannot be forgiven a debt of a million pounds and then demand that someone who owes him a few pounds must repay him. Of course, people can act like this (the servant in the parable, for example). But if they do they have not begun to grasp the privilege that has been extended to them. So it is in the kingdom of God.

We often speak of showing mercy. But what is mercy? Is it kindness, perhaps? Mercy includes kindness, but it is more than that. Someone has expressed the difference quaintly, but fairly accurately: kindness is a friend calling when you are well; mercy is a friend calling when you are sick.

The best illustration of the meaning of mercy is found in the parable of the Good Samaritan (*Lk. 10:30–37*). At the end of the parable Jesus asks which of three passers-by (a priest, a Levite, and a Samaritan) proved to be a neighbour to the man who was attacked by robbers. An expert in the law replied, 'The one who had mercy on him' (*Lk. 10:37*). The Samaritan illustrated the meaning of mercy.

Two things should be noted here about the Samaritan as an example of mercy.

1. *Mercy relieves the consequences of sin in the lives of others (both sinners and those sinned against).* The Samaritan took responsibility for the injured man. He ministered to his broken and bruised body and did everything he could to provide for restoration and healing. He did not deal with the cause of the man's need by chasing the robbers (it was not retribution he sought). He did not complain about the failure of society to meet the man's need (such protest was not the appropriate remedy for this man's condition). Rather, the Samaritan sought to work in the context of the immediate need set before him, and to bring relief.

Of course there is a place for seeking justice. And there is room for prophetic protest when society fails in its duty towards the needy. But neither of these things is the exercise of mercy. Mercy is getting down on your hands and knees and doing what you can to restore dignity to someone whose life has been broken by sin (whether his own or that of someone else).

[31]

No wonder the early church often used to think of *Jesus* himself as the Good Samaritan! When he encountered broken reeds, he did not break them; he healed them. When he met men whose lives were like dimly burning wicks, he did not quench them; he fanned them into flames. Jesus restored the weak and the bruised. He never passed them by, or worse, trampled on them (*Matt. 12:18–21*).

Are you like Jesus in this respect? Have you ever stopped for the sake of the bruised and broken? Or have you always found a reason to pass by on the other side (*Lk. 10:31,33*)?

2. *Mercy does not hide behind unbiblical scruples in order to protect itself from costly service.* The priest and the Levite who passed by the wounded man doubtless had their reasons for doing so. They had their own lives to attend to. They might turn the man over only to discover he was dead, and thus render themselves ritually unclean. How then could they get on with their 'ordinary routine'? Even though touching a dead body involved religious defilement, Jesus would have ignored it (*Lk. 7:14, 8:53–54*). Better to run the risk of becoming ritually unclean than to fail to show mercy to the needy! It is, after all, not a sin to be ritually unclean, but it is always sin to fail to show mercy.

What explains the merciless behaviour of the Levite and the priest? One reason was their refusal to pay the cost of being inconvenienced; another was their refusal to die to their own plans and to fit in with the providence of God in their lives. These things the Samaritan was prepared to do. In this respect, he was like Jesus.

Too often we underplay the importance of mercy in the Christian life. We treat it as an 'added extra,' perhaps even an 'optional extra.' But Scripture treats it as a divine necessity, which we ignore to our spiritual peril.

[32]

Mercy is not brought to light only by the New Testament. Did the priest and Levite not know God's word through Hosea: 'I desire mercy, not sacrifice, and acknowledgment of God rather than burnt offerings' (*Hos. 6:6*)? Surely they knew Micah 6:8: 'He has showed you, O man, what is good. And what does the Lord require of you? To act justly *and to love mercy* and to walk humbly with your God.'

Perhaps the most illuminating passage of all is to be found in Psalm 109. The striking thing about the psalm is the description of the psalmist's enemy: 'He never thought of doing a kindness [or showing mercy], but hounded to death the poor and the needy and the broken hearted. He found no pleasure in blessing' (*Ps. 109:16–17*).

This 'enemy' in Psalm 109 was seen in the New Testament as a picture of Judas Iscariot (see the quotation of *Psalm 109:8* in *Acts 2:20*). And there are traces of mercilessness in Judas's life. When Jesus was anointed with expensive perfume by Mary at Bethany, Judas complained bitterly, 'Why wasn't this perfume sold and the money given to the poor? . . .' He did not say this because he cared about the poor but because he was a thief; as keeper of the money bag, he used to help himself to what was put into it' (*Jn. 12:1–6*). He showed no mercy.

Lack of mercy is the mark of those who betray Jesus. Judas discovered, as Proverbs 21:13 teaches, 'If a man shuts his ears to the cry of the poor, he too will cry out and not be answered.' Judas was not merciful; he did not receive mercy.

Showing mercy to the poor and needy is a touchstone and hallmark of a true conversion to Christ. Without mercy, we are not Christ's, and he shall say to us on the last day (no matter what else we may have achieved), 'I never knew you. Away from me, you evildoers!' (*Matt. 7:23*).

How is it that we claim to be Christians, yet show so little mercy? Why are we so self-seeking, choosing a lifestyle of convenience rather than a self-sacrificing lifestyle of showing mercy? Is it because we have felt our own need of mercy far too little? Is it because we have only a superficial understanding of the riches of God's kindness to us? There can be no other explanations. Those who have been forgiven much, love much. Those who know they have received mercy, show mercy. And the merciful are greatly blessed, because they will receive mercy from God himself.

4
Purity, Peace, and Persecution

8'*Blessed are the pure in heart,*
    for they will see God.
9*Blessed are the peacemakers,*
    for they will be called sons of God.
10*Blessed are those who are persecuted*
    because of righteousness,
    for theirs is the kingdom of heaven.
        11'*Blessed are you when people insult you, persecute you*
and falsely say all kinds of evil against you because of me.
12*Rejoice and be glad, because great is your reward in heaven,*
for in the same way they persecuted the prophets who were
before you.'

*   *   *

You cannot choose which beatitudes you want to be true
of your life, and leave the others to one side. The
Beatitudes come as a whole, not as a series of options.
Every Christian is intended to show every grace. One

beatitude flows into the next, as we have already seen: the poor in spirit mourn for their sins, and as a result are marked by the meekness of those who know the truth about themselves in the presence of God. Such men and women hunger and thirst for righteousness, and receive it. Since they have been filled only because of the Lord's mercy to them, they become merciful to others.

Three further words of blessing follow – to the pure in heart, the peacemakers, and the persecuted. These beatitudes are also part of the sequence and belong in the rounded picture Jesus is giving us of the mature disciple. As we become pure in heart (the meaning of which we will examine more carefully), we see God. But he is the God of peace (*1 Thess. 5:23; Heb. 13:20*), through the blood of the Cross (*Col. 1:20*). To see who he is, is to have a desire to bring others into his peace. The pure in heart are, therefore, also peacemakers. But what do they discover? Like Jesus, they are persecuted. Yet they can rejoice, because this numbers them with the prophets of Christ who were persecuted before them.

PURITY OF HEART

Who are the pure in heart? At first glance, Jesus seems to be thinking here about those whose hearts are morally clean. Undoubtedly, his words have Ezekiel's prophecy as their background: 'I will sprinkle clean water on you, and you will be clean; I will cleanse you from all your impurities and from all your idols. I will give you a new heart and put a new spirit in you' (*Ez. 36:25–26*).

Yet this purity, of which the Old Testament speaks, is not only a matter of cleanliness (although it involves such) but also a matter of the commitment of the heart and will to the Lord.

The background for that statement lies in Psalm 24:4–6.

Those who may stand in the Lord's holy presence have 'clean hands and a pure heart.' They have not lifted up their souls to an idol. (Notice the same emphasis in Ezekiel's words.) The impurity involved here is the impurity of compromise and accommodation. The impure heart is not simply unclean; it is *undecided* and *divided*. It is characteristic of the man James describes as 'double-minded' (*Ja. 1:8; 4:8*) and, therefore, unstable in all his ways.

The Danish theologian-philosopher Søren Kierkegaard expressed Jesus' meaning well in the title of one of his books: *Purity of heart is to will one thing*. To be pure in heart is to be uncompromisingly dedicated to Christ! This is the way truly to see (or 'know') God.

Being pure in heart means letting nothing stand in the way of our vision of Christ. He is a great Saviour and Lord. But great things can be completely obscured by small things if the small things are brought near enough to our eyes. The issue, therefore, is not how important something is in itself, but how closely we fix our gaze upon it. We see that this world has nothing to compare to Jesus Christ and all that he offers to us. But when we hold this world and its contents too near, we no longer see Christ and his glory so clearly. The value of this world grows out of proportion. We compromise, stumble, and fall.

Jesus' teaching here provides us with a simple test of the strength of our Christian lives. *How clearly do we see God in all his glory?* Do we see him as clearly as we used to? Or has he become obscure and distant? Have we maintained the sharpness of our vision of him through whole-hearted commitment to him? Are we pure in heart?

PEACEMAKING

Jesus says that peacemakers enter into his covenant blessing. They will be called the sons of God. Jesus' logic is

S.O.M.—4

not difficult to follow. God is described in Scripture as the God of peace. As such, he has made peace for us through Christ; he has reconciled us to himself (*2 Cor. 5:19–21*). Making peace is part of God's gracious character. Those who have become members of his family will share in his family likeness. His sons will be peacemakers.

Like the other beatitudes, this one has been wrested out of its context many times. Jesus is not speaking about the mere cessation of hostilities among the nations. He is speaking about the cessation of hostilities between man and God. This is the peace he came to establish.

The Old Testament word for peace is *shalom*. It is a rich word, and conveys the idea of wholeness, health, well-being. It could almost be translated 'salvation.' Those who make peace are those who earnestly seek the *shalom*, the salvation, of their fellows.

Hidden logically in what Jesus says about peacemakers is a recurrent thought in the New Testament: evangelism is not an option – something in which a few members of every fellowship are expected to show an interest. Evangelism (in whatever form) is an integral part of being a Christian.

How can this be deduced from what Jesus says? Very simply. Those who make peace are called sons of God. Since all Christians are sons of God, all Christians are expected to share in the work of peacemaking.

That is not to say we are all equally well-equipped for all aspects of personal evangelism. It means only that all of us share in the responsibility of living lives and speaking words that contribute to the conversion of others. Paul saw that as one of the debts we owe to the world (*Rom. 1:14*). The Christian church would be healthier (and happier, being more conscious that we are sons of God!) if it shared Paul's conviction.

There is another dimension to the peacemaking activities of the children of God. The sons of God will seek peace *among themselves*, in the fellowship of the family of God.

That is very often part of a minister's vows when he is installed. He promises to keep 'the peace of the church.' It seems easy to say, but the fact of the matter is that it is very challenging. Many churches are destroyed because the members, or leaders, shirk their responsibility precisely here. They do not regard the work of peacemaking to be appropriate for them. They forget that those who destroy God's temple will be destroyed by God (*I Cor. 3:17*). Their own wisdom and their own ways are more important than God's will, which is for peace and harmony among his people.

Of course, there are occasions when error has to be rooted out, and men have to take their stand on the truth of the gospel. But is it not strange that the churches that experience a great deal of disruption are often those that most loudly proclaim allegiance to God's infallible word?

Are bitterness and strife strangers in evangelical fellowships? Alas, no! They were not absent in Rome, or Corinth, or even Philippi in the first century. And they continue to rear their ugly heads in our fellowships today. Too often the causes are pride and the desire for power and position. How slow we are to learn that we are a family, and that the Father's will is that we should live together in harmony.

Paul used two marvellous word pictures to underline Jesus' teaching. In Colossians 3:15 Paul writes, 'Let the peace of Christ rule in your hearts, since as members of one body you were called to peace.' We can pictorialise his statement: Peace is the referee who blows the whistle on any action that is out of line. Paul does not mean that we are to feel peace deep down. Whether we do or not is

[39]

beside the point. Rather, he means that God has called us to peace. Therefore, peace, the harmony and well-being of our fellowship, must have priority. We will subordinate other considerations (our will, our position, our natural desires) to the *shalom* of our fellowship.

Some Christians never do that. They do not seem to know or care that Jesus prayed that his people might dwell in unity as he and his Father did (*Jn. 17:20–1*). To disrupt peace in a church fellowship is to despise both the prayers of Christ and the blessing of Christ.

In Ephesians 4:3, Paul uses another word picture. In the context of urging us to practice humility, patience, and forbearance, he adds, 'Make every effort to keep the unity of the Spirit through the bond of peace.' Peace is the bond – the 'cord' – that ties us all together. By nature and by instinct, we would never act as one body. But God's peace can accomplish that.

John Owen, the Puritan, uses a fine illustration: Imagine a man collecting wood for his fireplace. He finds a good supply of branches, but they are of varied shapes and sizes: some long and thin, others short and thick; some straight, others twisted. He binds them together with a rope, and in one bundle easily carries them home.

So it is in the Church. What a varied bunch we are! How will Christ carry us home? He ties us together with the bond of peace! Cut that bond, and you cut the cord Christ himself has tied.

Can you honestly say that you have faithfully sought the peace of Christ's church?

PERSECUTION

The climax to the Beatitudes almost seems to be an anti-climax. It takes us back to where we started – the promise of the kingdom of God. We are told that we will be persecuted. Perhaps Jesus realised how surprising this might seem to his disciples, so he emphasised his point by applying it directly to his followers.

Is this the reverse of what we would expect? Men and women who are poor in spirit, mourn for their sin, live lives of gracious meekness, long for God's righteousness, show mercy to others, are pure in heart, and seek peace between God and man – would such people not be welcomed with open arms? After all, these are the very men and women the world needs!

The world in which we live assumes that it will welcome Christians with open arms – until the first time it meets the genuine article. Until then, it is ignorant of its real response to the gospel. It assumes that it is well-disposed to Jesus Christ and to God.

But Scripture tell us otherwise: the world is in rebellion against God. Jesus himself said that if men persecuted him, they would also persecute his followers (*Jn. 15:20*). He told them, 'If the world hates you, keep in mind that it hated me first' (*Jn. 15:18*).

Christians are persecuted for the sake of righteousness because of their loyalty to Christ. Real loyalty to him creates friction in the hearts of those who pay him only lip service. Loyalty arouses their consciences, and leaves them with only two alternatives: follow Christ, or silence him. Often their only way of silencing Christ is by silencing his servants. Persecution, in subtle or less subtle forms, is the result.

We have already seen that the gospel produces a lifestyle characterised by righteousness. In practice, that means absolute integrity, whether at home, in the work place, or even at play. But such integrity challenges the moral indifference of the world, not least in our own age. Not to do the things 'everybody does' stirs the world's sleepy conscience. More than that, it irritates it, and causes annoyance and even anger.

You would not think that simple honesty could be a dangerous lifestyle, until you put it into practice on the shop floor! For the Christian who is employed by another person, righteousness demands that he give his employer the time and energy for which he is paid. It means moral integrity. But how angry other employees can be when such integrity is displayed!

At the beginning of the Christian life, we need to grasp the reality of persecution. This awareness will save us from discouragement and disillusionment. We follow a *crucified* Saviour. We should not think it strange if we ourselves encounter fiery trials (*1 Pet. 4:12*). Rather, we should learn to rejoice that we have been counted worthy to suffer for the name of Christ (*Acts 5:41*). Ours is the kingdom of God!

This, then, is the life of divine blessing. Do you know it? If not, let William Cowper's words become your words:

> *Where is the blessedness I knew*
> *When first I saw the Lord?*
> *Where is the soul-refreshing view*
> *Of Jesus and his word?*
>
> *Return O Holy Dove! return*
> *Sweet messenger of rest!*
> *I hate the sins that made Thee mourn,*
> *And drove Thee from my breast.*
>
> *The dearest idol I have known,*
> *Whate'er that idol be,*
> *Help me to tear it from Thy throne,*
> *And worship only Thee.*
>
> *So shall my walk be close with God,*
> *Calm and serene my frame;*
> *So purer light shall mark the road*
> *That leads me to the Lamb.*

5
Future Blessings Now

¹*Now when he saw the crowds, he went up on a mountainside and sat down. His disciples came to him, ²and he began to teach them, saying:*
   ³*'Blessed are the poor in spirit,*
      for theirs is the kingdom of heaven.
   ⁴*Blessed are those who mourn,*
      for they will be comforted.
   ⁵*Blessed are the meek,*
      for they will inherit the earth.
   ⁶*Blessed are those who hunger and*
         thirst for righteousness,
      for they will be filled.
   ⁷*Blessed are the merciful,*
      for they will be shown mercy.
   ⁸*Blessed are the pure in heart,*
      for they will see God.
   ⁹*Blessed are the peacemakers,*
      for they will be called sons of God.
   ¹⁰*Blessed are those who are persecuted*

because of righteousness,
for theirs is the kingdom of heaven.
[11]*'Blessed are you when people insult you, persecute you
and falsely say all kinds of evil against you because of me.*
[12]*Rejoice and be glad, because great is your reward in heaven,
for in the same way they persecuted the prophets who were
before you.'*

*   *   *

In the previous three chapters, we have focused most of
our attention on the characteristic marks and lifestyle of
those who experience the blessings, or beatitudes, of the
kingdom of God. It was important to do so because, as
Christians, many of us fail to be the kind of men and
women God wants us to be – decided disciples, expressing
the life and grace of our Lord Jesus Christ himself.

Yet, to emphasise only the character of those who know
the Lord's blessings would be to truncate Jesus' teaching
in the Sermon on the Mount. He is not, after all, telling us
what we should be. Rather, he is describing *what the power
of God's kingdom makes us.* Jesus assumes that his people
will show these hallmarks. But because they are so
contrary to our natural dispositions, he wants to stress that
this really is the way to blessing. It is not the rich, the
happy, the forceful, the merciless, who are truly blessed.
It is the poor in spirit, the meek, those who hunger and
thirst for righteousness because they see their lack of it;
these alone know God's blessing, and as a result, his many
Beatitudes!

So, it is important that we should think further about
the blessing that Jesus promises to us. When we look at
the blessings, we discover the reason it is appropriate to
consider them together, as we plan to do in this chapter.
They belong together, as parts of a whole. Just as all the

[44]

marks of the kingdom's presence must be seen in our lives, so the blessings of the Beatitudes belong together.

Jesus himself makes this plain by beginning and ending the Beatitudes with the same promised blessing: 'Theirs is the kingdom of heaven' (*v. 3 and 10*). In verses 4–9, this chief blessing is further explained and illustrated in a series of six specific blessings: comfort (*v. 4*), inheriting the earth (*v. 5*), being filled (*v. 6*), receiving mercy (*v. 7*), seeing God (*v. 8*), and being called sons of God (*v. 9*).

In its simplest terms, Jesus' teaching means this: his disciples have already – here and now – entered into the kingdom. Yes, it is still to be consummated. Yes, it is still to be revealed in its final glory. Yes, we still wait for the day when loud voices will say, 'The kingom of the world has become the kingdom of our Lord and of his Christ, and he will reign for ever and ever' (*Rev. 11:15*). Nevertheless, all the blessings that are expected in that kingdom *in the future,* are *already* being experienced by Christ's people *now*!

Paul puts this idea in a slightly different form when he writes to the Christians at Ephesus, a city dominated by the sins of the kingdom of this world. Yet, the Ephesian Christians belong to another King – Jesus. The air they breathe, spiritually speaking, belongs to the city of God. Their 'light and power' come from their fellowship with him. They are 'in Christ Jesus' as well as 'in Ephesus' (*Eph. 1:1*). So Paul writes to them that God 'has blessed us in the heavenly realms with every spiritual blessing in Christ' (*Eph. 1:3*).

In his first letter to the Christians at Corinth, Paul tells them they have been rescued from 'the present evil age' (*Gal. 1:4*), and brought into the life of the 'age to come' (*1 Cor. 10:11*). In other words, they – and we – already share in the powers of the kingdom of heaven!

[45]

To those who first heard Jesus teach the Beatitudes, the meaning was: 'The future is now. The reign of God, with its blessings, which you expected to come at the end of the age and the close of history, has arrived in the here and now. Enter my kingdom. Experience its life-changing power. Taste the blessings of the future *now*!'

Izaak Walton, writer (best known as the author of the seventeenth-century fishing manual, *The Compleat Angler*), wrote of one of his great Christian contemporaries, Richard Sibbes,

> *Of this blest man,*
> *Let this just praise be given:*
> *Heaven was in him*
> *Before he was in heaven.*

But these quaint lines are just as true of every Christian, for we have already received the heavenly Spirit as the guarantee that we will fully enter into our inheritance (*Eph. 1:13–14*). The Christian life is not 'the opiate of the people,' dulling our senses now in the hope of better things hereafter. Rather, says Jesus, it is blessing now and more blessing to come!

What, then, are these blessings shared by those of whom Jesus says, 'Theirs is the kingdom of heaven'?

COMFORT FOR THE MOURNING

Through the prophet Isaiah, the Lord had promised comfort (strength, vitality) to his people in exile. The second half of that prophecy envisages God's people in captivity to the kingdom of this world. It pictures God bringing about a new exodus of his people and leading them back into the promised land. And so it begins, 'Comfort, comfort my people' (*Is. 40:1*).

In Isaiah 61:1–3 (the entire passage seems to lie behind the Beatitudes), this promise reaches its climax in the words of the coming Messiah:

The Spirit of the Sovereign Lord is on me,
*   because the Lord has anointed me*
to preach good news to the poor. . . .
*   to bind up the brokenhearted, . . .*
to comfort all who mourn,
*   and provide for those who grieve in Zion –*
to bestow on them a crown of beauty
*   instead of ashes,*
the oil of gladness
*   instead of mourning,*
and a garment of praise
*   instead of a spirit of despair.*

These words were fulfilled in Jesus. He read them in the synagogue in Nazareth, and added, 'Today this scripture is fulfilled in your hearing' (*Lk. 4:16–21*). The blessings of the new exodus are ours in Christ. (In Luke 9:31, the author uses the Greek word *exodus* in reference to Jesus' death and resurrection.)

Our mourning over sin involves our sense of guilt and shame, our experience of regret and separation from God. But Jesus Christ is the One who lifts up the heads of his people (*Ps. 3:3*). He comes to us in his grace and power, puts his hand under our chin, and says, 'Lift up your eyes, sorrowing one; look on me. I am the Resurrection and the Life. In me there is forgiveness and pardon. Through me you are being brought into fellowship with the Father. You need not carry the burden of mourning through life, hoping against hope that one day it will be removed. No! I have taken that burden. There is comfort now. Put aside the garments of mourning. Rejoice! Be comforted!'

Jesus illustrated this beatitude in his parable of the Pharisee and the tax collector. He pictured both men at prayer. The Pharisee spoke publicly and proudly of his achievements. No mourning for him! By contrast, the tax collector was too ashamed to lift up his eyes to heaven. He stood at a distance from everyone else, beat his breast, and said, 'God, have mercy on me, a (literally 'the') sinner' (*Lk. 18:13*). Jesus said the tax collector went home justified before God.

Can you imagine the stunned silence among the hearers? Jesus had obviously bungled the punch-line of his story.

On the contrary! He was speaking to 'some who were confident of their own righteousness and looked down on everybody else' (*Lk. 18:9*). Jesus was teaching that the man who mourns over his sin – contrary to all expectation – is not condemned, but pardoned. That is blessedness beyond anyone's expectation.

THE INHERITANCE OF THE MEEK

When God made man, he created him to rule over the earth as his steward. God gave man dominion over everything (*Gen. 1:26–28*). But man wanted more, and succumbed to the serpent's temptation: 'You will be like God, knowing good and evil' (*Gen. 3:5*. The second phrase seems to mean 'able to decide things for yourself.').

The fall of man had begun. Made to rule the world for God, he tried to seize it for himself. As a consequence, he lost what he tried to steal and also the dignity that God had given to him. Instead of bowing in meekness before his gracious Master, as God's creature and son should do, man arrogantly tried to usurp the place of God.

In the fragments of revelation God gave to his ancient people, he included various hints that one day this tragedy would be reversed. So, in the Old Testament promises he had included the gift of 'the land' to Israel. Sometimes they proudly viewed the land as their right, irrespective of whether they lived in it with meekness before God. Time and time again, God had to teach them that pride always loses what it seeks to gain. The fact that their leader was the meekest man on the earth (*Numb. 12:3*) should have taught them a great lesson, especially since he was denied entry into the Promised Land because he abandoned that meekness at a critical juncture (*Numb. 20:12*).

Jesus was – and is – meek and humble in heart (*Matt. 11:29*). He submitted himself to the will of God and to the harsh experiences that were to fall on the Suffering Servant. That is why he was able to say to his disciples that all authority in heaven and earth was – and is – his (*Matt. 28:18*). Now, through the mission of the church, he is claiming what is his by right: not just the promised land of Palestine, but the whole earth (*see Ps. 2:8 and Heb. 2:5–9*).

One day this sovereign rule of Jesus will be seen publicly. For the moment, it is seen only through the eyes of faith. But because it *is* seen by the eyes of faith, the people of God already have the assurance that this earth belongs to Christ; he has won it back for his people. He wants them to be his stewards again! This is partly what Paul means when he writes:

> *In my opinion whatever we may have to go through now is less than nothing compared with the magnificent future God has planned for us. The whole creation is on tiptoe to see the wonderful sight of the sons of God coming into their own.* (Rom. 8:18, Phillips)

But even now, the Christian has a partial experience of this. He knows that, despite its fallen state and in view of its future transformation, this world is not his enemy. It is no longer the lonely (even sinister) place it once was to

[49]

him. It is God's world, and God has promised to transform it – and to transform him, to make him fit to live in God's world as his inheritance.

We can enjoy God's creation without being its prisoners! Since we will inherit the earth, we can live now as stewards of the earth, meekly submitting to the purpose of our Father in heaven.

FILLED WITH RIGHTEOUSNESS

Christ promises that those who hunger and thirst for righteousness will be *filled*, or *satisfied* (*Matt. 5:6*). We have already seen that this righteousness means 'right relationships' – with God, with others, and with ourselves. Jesus' promise indicates that we will know these now, not only in the 'new heavens and a new earth,' when 'the wolf and the lamb will feed together, and the lion will eat straw like the ox, but dust will be the serpent's food' (*Is. 65:17,25*). These right relationships will mark the entire reign of God's Messiah, from its beginning (*Is. 11:1–9; Lk. 1:75*). Already we are justified by faith, or 'right-wised,' as it has been put (*Rom. 5:1*). Already we know that the kingdom of God consists of righteousness (*Rom. 14:17*). Already we are being filled with the fruit of righteousness that comes through Jesus Christ (*Phil. 1:11*)!

Those who are full of righteousness will be persecuted because of it (*Matt. 5:10*). But along with that persecution, Jesus gives the promise of blessing: 'I tell you the truth, . . . no one who has left home or wife or brothers or parents or children for the sake of the kingdom of God will fail to receive many times as much *in this age* and, in the age to come, eternal life' (*Lk. 18:29*).

This is what Jesus means when he says in the sermon that everything we need will be provided for us if we make the kingdom and the righteousness of God our first priority

(*Matt. 6:33*). Millions of Christians throughout the ages can bear witness to the certainty of his promise.

He fills us with right relationships. We have God as our Father, and the people of God as our family: fathers and mothers to guide and help us; brothers and sisters to stand beside us; sons and daughters to care for and encourage. In every tribe and tongue and nation, God will have his people, and they will all be our family. In our own Christian spheres, we experience the restoration of true fellowship and friendship. We enter into a caring, loving, healing, serving community where right and restored relationships can take place. These positive relationships may be only a foretaste of what is yet to be. But what a glorious foretaste it is!

RECEIVING MERCY

We have seen that mercy is God stooping down to man in his weakness and inability, to bring him healing and restoration. He is the Good Samaritan, binding the wounds, carrying the burdens, and providing for the recovery of the man who was attacked by robbers (*Lk. 10:33-35*). This is what God does for us in Jesus Christ.

The letter to the Hebrews describes Jesus as 'a merciful and faithful high priest' (*Heb. 2:17*). To become such, Jesus was made like us in every way. As a result, 'because he himself suffered when he was tempted, he is able to help those who are being tempted' (*Heb. 2:18*).

The merciful will receive mercy (*Matt. 5:7*). Think about what this beatitude means. Unlike the priest in the parable of the Good Samaritan, who was unwilling to take the risk of being defiled, the Son of God came to share in our weakness, and even to experience our temptations. He knows what it is like because he has experienced what we go through. In fact, because he withstood every temptation, he has felt their force to the full. But why did he do this? In order 'to help those who are being tempted'!

God's mercy in Christ helps us to our feet when we have fallen, and defends and protects us when we are weak and helpless. God's mercy pours the oil of healing into the wounds in our conscience, our heart, our memories, and our personality. God's mercy supplies the place of rest and encouragement we need, in the fellowship of his people (Jude wrote to the early Christians, 'Be merciful to those who doubt' [*Jude 22*]). At the last day, this same God will bring final healing and restoration when he transforms us into the image of Christ (*Phil. 3:20–21; 1 Jn. 3:2*). The Lord's mercy is from everlasting to everlasting!

SEEING GOD

The pure in heart – those who desire both to know and serve him – will see God (*Matt. 5:8*). What can this mean? Scripture tells us that no man has ever seen God because he is the invisible God (*Jn. 1:18; Col. 1:15; 1 Tim. 1:17; Heb. 11:27*). How, then, can the pure in heart see him? Does Jesus mean that in some new way, in heaven, we will 'see God'?

The clue to understanding what it means to see God probably lies in those Old Testament passages that describe the experiences of those who are 'pure in heart.' *Psalm 24:3–6* indicates that the pure in heart have the privilege of ascending the hill of the Lord and entering into the presence of God in his holy place. They seek God and receive blessing from him. *Psalm 73:1* states that God is good to those who are pure in heart. In verses 24–28 of that psalm, Asaph (the author) tells us how he came to this conclusion: 'You guide me with your counsel, and afterward you will take me into glory. . . . As for me, it is good to be near God.'

Both of these passages emphasise the privileges and joys of conscious fellowship with God and the knowledge that we are in his presence. These passages refer to the day when the people of God will be brought into his glory, into an even more profound sense of his nearness and holiness.

Occasionally – in unusual visions – Old Testament prophets like Isaiah 'saw the Lord seated on a throne, high and exalted' (*Is. 6:1*). Ezekiel saw 'the appearance of the likeness of the glory of the Lord' (*Ezek. 1:28*). These were glimpses of the unveiling that is yet to take place. Even in the Old Testament, the pure in heart were promised that they would 'see God.'

Jesus confirms this, but he also develops it further. The blessing of belonging to the kingdom of God is this: in some measure, that long-hoped-for day of the vision of God has already arrived. In the words of John, 'We have seen his glory, the glory of the one and only Son, who came from the Father, full of grace and truth' (*Jn. 1:14*). When Philip said to Jesus, 'Lord, show us the Father and that will be enough for us,' Jesus' answer was, 'Don't you know me, Philip, even after I have been among you such a long time? Anyone who has seen me has seen the Father' (*Jn. 14:8–9*).

In Jesus, God makes himself visible. But his identity remains hidden to those with divided hearts. Only those whose hearts are purified by faith 'see' him as he really is. To know Christ is to know God and to 'see' him (*Jn. 17:3*). It means experiencing the vision of God now, and tasting his glory. That is why Peter, who had seen God's glory on the Mount of Transfiguration, wrote that the Spirit of glory and of God rests on Christians (*1 Pet. 4:14*). The future sense of the Lord's presence is *already* ours. Like Moses – but in a fuller sense – we see him who is invisible, and learn to persevere to the end. Then we will see his glory in a yet clearer way (*Heb. 11:27*).

CALLED SONS OF GOD

The Beatitudes are not haphazard in their order. They begin and end with the assurance that the kingdom of heaven is ours through Jesus Christ. But giving reasons for the order is not at all easy. If it were, commentators would have offered fewer explanations of it!

The ultimate blessing is to be called a son of the living God. Does this seem to be an anticlimax after the promise that we shall see God? In fact, it is a wonderful climax, for there is no higher privilege we could ever experience than this – to see God *as our Father*. The blessing implies that in the kingdom of God we are restored to what we were meant to be – children of God (*cf. Lk. 3:38*). We see him as children who love and trust their Father, and who know that he will supply all their needs.

Jesus develops this point at great length in the middle section of his challenging sermon. Being aware of this particular blessing will set us free, he says, from both hypocrisy and paralysing anxiety about temporal concerns. Best of all, since sons inherit their father's riches as well as their father's characteristics, this beatitude summarises all the beatitudes. It tells us that God speaks to us in these words:

> *My son, . . . you are always with me, and everything I have is yours.* (Lk. 15:31)

Blessed, indeed, is the man or woman who has heard God say that!

6
The Christian in the World

[13]*'You are the salt of the earth. But if the salt loses its saltiness, how can it be made salty again? It is no longer good for anything, except to be thrown out and trampled by men.*

[14]*'You are the light of the world. A city on a hill cannot be hidden.* [15]*Neither do people light a lamp and put it under a bowl. Instead they put it on its stand, and it gives light to everyone in the house.* [16]*In the same way, let your light shine before men, that they may see your good deeds and praise your Father in heaven.'*

★　　★　　★

The kingdom of God has come in the person of Jesus Christ. But its power and influence are visible only in the sphere in which the world least expects to see them – in the poor in spirit, among those who mourn over sin, and in the persecuted community of the followers of Jesus. It is these who receive the divine benediction.

The Beatitudes come to a climax with a clear hint at the

conflict that exists between the kingdom of God and the kingdoms of this world. There is opposition to Christ's people, and even persecution of them. The true church is too different for the world to tolerate it. The world sees the kingdom of God as a threat to its own ways, and so it seeks to destroy it.

If this is the response of the world to the kingdom of God, how are those who belong to the kingdom to live in the world? And how can they live in a way that will make an impact for God's glory among men? It is to these questions that Jesus now turns his attention in the course of his exposition.

He uses two pictures drawn from the everyday world of his time to illustrate what it means to be a Christian in a pagan society: Christians are like salt; Christians are like light. What salt and light were to life in first-century Palestine, Christians are to the society in which they live.

THE SALT OF THE EARTH

What did Jesus mean when he said that Christians are salt? Notice that he said, '*You are* the salt of the earth.' The mood of the verb is indicative (a statement of fact), not imperative (a command to be something). Jesus is not urging his disciples to become something they are not; he is telling them what they are as kingdom people. The implication is that they are to be what God has thus made them.

Jesus is speaking in the context of the persecution of his disciples. Like salt, Christians may seem small and insignificant, powerless in a power-mad society. Yet they have the ability to influence every segment of it and to permeate the whole. Salt is cheap; its value is minimal. But salt has unusual properties that far exceed its 'value.' So it is with the members of God's kingdom. Like salt, there will be times when their true usefulness will become very clear.

More obvious, however, is the fact that in Jesus' day salt was a vital preservative. Even in the modern world, we are familiar with its use to preserve meat, to keep it from spoiling. I recall being introduced to a traditional delicacy in South Africa known as 'biltong,' small thin strips of meat that had been salted and dried. Long-distance travellers in past generations had carried biltong with them. So successfully preserved was it, that such meat almost did not need a 'best-eaten-by' date!

The point needs little explanation. But it calls for radical and costly application. Christians whose lives exhibit the qualities of the 'blessed' will have a preserving impact upon a society that, if left to itself, will rot and deteriorate. Without the influence of the gospel, society will suffer moral decay and become putrid, unfit for the consumption of good men and women.

Two other biblical uses of salt carry this same principle a little further. Ezekiel 16:4 hints at the Jewish practice of rubbing newborn babies with salt. In all likelihood, this practice was not for ritual cleanliness, but for hygiene. Already it was understood that if hygiene was ignored at the beginning of life, sickness and even death could result.

If this practice was in our Lord's mind, the application of his illustration would be this: commit yourself to being salt in your society at the earliest possible opportunity. Be willing to pay whatever price needs to be paid in terms of the world's response. It is important, if our lives are to make a moral impact on others, that we live as Christians among them and take our stand right from the very start.

This same principle is further illustrated in Judges 9:45. When Abimelech defeated the city of Shechem, 'he destroyed the city and scattered salt over it.' The use of salt was a symbolic and perhaps also an effective action, to render the ground infertile for the future.

This is precisely what the Christian does when he takes his stand for God in society; he makes that society, be it his friends in school, his fellow students at college, his co-workers, or those with whom he plays sports, less fertile soil for other ungodly influences. Of course, that in itself will not regenerate his society, but it will make it more difficult for sinful attitudes and habits and words to become the norm among his friends and colleagues.

I have a friend who was awarded a distinguished medal for his contribution to a famous effort of exploration. His medal was for scientific research and the advance of knowledge. But that was not, in the long run, his greatest contribution to the exploration team. It was said of him that 'he kept the party *clean*.'

It is all too easy for us to despair as Christians because of our frailty and insignificance, personally or numerically. However, we must never give in to Satan's lie that we can be effective only when we have large numbers and a show of strength. Jesus' illustration of salt is an encouraging reminder that the apparently cheap and insignificant can influence its environment out of all proportion to our expectation.

Sometimes this happens on a national scale. It is said, with some justification, that the only thing that saved England from a revolution as horrible and bloody as the French Revolution was the evangelical revival under the preaching and teaching of men like John Wesley and George Whitefield during the eighteenth century.

More frequently it will happen on a small scale: your companions will moderate their language; the name of Jesus will not be so easily blasphemed; those with whom you work will develop something of a conscience about the standard of their work; the conversations of men or women will be brought under control; respect for others will be more common. Your life will save others from yielding to the immoral pressures by which our contemporary world is characterised. *When you are the salt of the earth, you preserve society.*

We are familiar with another property of salt: it not only preserves, but it also *seasons*. It brings out the flavour. According to *The Oxford English Dictionary*, one meaning of the word *season* is 'give zest to.' Christians should have zest!

Jesus surely has this in mind also. 'Seasoning' society is not a matter of being Scrooge-like personalities whose presence brings a pall of depression and whose entrance marks the exit of joy. On the contrary, the presence of God's people should 'increase the flavour' of life in many different ways. After all, we come to our friends, neighbours, co-workers, or fellow students as those who have been – and still are – in the presence of Jesus Christ, who has given us abundant life (*Jn. 10:10*). Everything about us should express the attractiveness as well as the holiness of our Lord.

Jesus himself had this 'zest.' By his very presence he raised the spirits of people. Of course, there came a parting of the ways with those who would not follow him, but even they knew that there was a quality about his life that could not be explained in natural terms.

Nor was this zest the cheap and tawdry and often egocentric 'joy' or 'charisma' we sometimes encounter today masquerading as Christianity. Jesus' attractiveness did not draw attention to itself. It did not need to, because it was genuine. You do not need to draw attention to real quality; it speaks for itself.

Paul tells us that our *speech* in particular should be seasoned with salt (*Col. 4:6*). He explains what he means

[59]

in the parallel passage, (in *Eph. 4:29*): 'Do not let any unwholesome talk come out of your mouths, but only what is helpful for building others up according to their needs, that it may benefit those who listen.'

Interestingly, it is in this context that Paul urges us not to grieve the Holy Spirit. Why in this context? Because our speech is one of the best measurements of the condition of our spirit. And just as it can do much harm (see *Jas. 3:3–12*), so our speech can be the vehicle of great blessing: it can help others and build them up by its appropriateness (*Eph. 4:29*); it can lift the spirits of the discouraged; it can put the whole of life in a new perspective. Most of all, it is the vehicle by which Christ is made known – but notice, not only by what we say, but by *how* we say it.

Speech is like salt: too little, and we do not taste the flavour of the food; too much, and we are left with the unpleasant taste of the salt. Like salt, our lives and our speech are to bring out the 'flavour' of Jesus Christ. Too much of ourselves – too much of our talk – will likewise leave an unpleasant taste. Be like Christ, then, lest others are not able to tell the difference between the salt and the meat, between the poverty of our witness and the goodness of the Lord Jesus they are invited to taste (*Ps. 34:8*).

One further use of salt in Jesus' culture may have been in his mind as he used this illustration. Sacrifices were accompanied with salt, described as 'the salt of the covenant of your God' (*Lev. 2:13*). This salt of the covenant was a *symbol of faithfulness*. The fact that God commanded his people to include it probably means that it was intended as a symbol of their response, a sign that the sacrifices were offered with hearts set on knowing and serving the Lord.

In the last analysis, this is what makes the Christian different! He is faithful, both to his Lord and to others. He can be trusted. He is like Joseph in the court of Pharaoh, Daniel in the court of Nebuchadnezzar, and John the

Baptist in the court of King Herod. The Christian is different – sometimes frustratingly, annoyingly, maddeningly different – but he is also the only one who ultimately can be trusted to tell the whole truth. This is what it means to be the salt of the earth.

When salt loses its saltiness, it is worthless. Jesus says that it should be thrown out and become part of the pathway (*Matt. 5:13*). Instead of influencing men's taste, it is trodden under their feet. The same is true for those of us who profess to be Christians. Cease to be different, and we cease to be Christians.

How slow we often are to learn this lesson. At times we fall into the trap of being blackmailed by a world that says, 'Unless I find your life attractive *on my own terms*, I will not respond to the message of the gospel.' But if we yield at that point, we become prisoners to perpetual blackmail.

I have sometimes heard Christians witness to people in these terms: 'You mustn't think being a Christian takes away your fun. I can enjoy doing the same things you do. Being a Christian isn't a series of don'ts!' Much of this may be true, but why should the church be so concerned to tell the world that it is not really very different from the world? The church then becomes both powerless and pointless.

Jesus emphasises that our ability to preserve the world in order that it may see Christ in us *depends* on our being different. That does not mean the Christian will always be saying, 'Look at me. I'm different.' No, instead he 'lets' his light shine before men; he does not need to switch it on and off to draw attention to the fact that he is unashamedly different.

Someone has expressed this point in these words: Jesus told us to be fishers of men, not frogmen! We are to live in this world, to witness to men and women; we are not to be out of sight beneath the surface. If we have no moral 'bite' in the different quality of our lifestyle, then we are no longer salt in the world.

This is exactly the point of Jesus' prayer in John 17:15–19. He does not pray that we will be taken out of the world (how, then, could we be his witnesses in it?). Instead, he prays that we will be kept holy so that when we are sent into the world, we will show Christ to it.

How is this possible? What is it that helps Christians retain their 'saltiness'? In praying to his Father, Jesus explains, 'I have given them your word and the world has hated them, for they are not of the world any more than I am of the world. . . . Sanctify them by the truth; your word is truth' (*Jn. 17:14,17*).

One part of the 'word' Jesus gave his disciples is the teaching in the Sermon on the Mount. It has the power to make us salt in the world, and to keep us sharp and faithful in our service to Jesus. As we open our lives to the impact of the whole of Scripture, with its message of a whole Christ, then the whole of our lives will begin to radiate his saving power and grace.

THE LIGHT OF THE WORLD

Jesus' second description of his people is that they are the light of the world.

Jesus himself is the light of the world (*Jn. 8:12*), the great light who has come to the people living in darkness (*Matt. 4:16*). Those who belong to him are brought out of the kingdom of darkness into his kingdom of light (*Col. 1:12–13*). As a result, we, too, have become 'light in the Lord' and are to live as children of the light, having nothing to do with the deeds of darkness (*Eph. 5:8–14*). Instead, we are to expose such deeds by the light that our own lives shine on the moral darkness around us.

In explaining what he means, Jesus uses two further pictures. The first is a city that cannot be hidden because it stands prominently on a hill. The second is a light that ought not to be hidden because it is intended to give light to people in a house.

Even in our modern age of sophisticated refrigerators and freezers, we still understand the effect of salt – or lack of it – with our meals. But unless we have experienced rural life, it may be a little more difficult for us emotionally to appreciate the concept of darkness. City dwellers in the modern world rarely, if ever, experience total darkness.

I lived at one time on the most northerly island in the United Kingdom. It was the island on which Robert Louis Stevenson modelled his famous *Treasure Island*. So far north was the island that in the winter the sun did not rise until about 9 o'clock in the morning, and it began to set around 3 o'clock in the afternoon. Then darkness descended. And what darkness! It was impossible to see the fingers on one's hand, or the features of someone near enough to touch. Conversation in the dark could be an eerie experience!

By contrast, if one lives in the general proximity of a city today, there will always be the glow of light in the sky. If that city happens to be set on a hill, the light will be visible for many miles, and will lighten the darkness all around.

No doubt those listening to Jesus lived in rural communities. They were familiar with what darkness really meant, and with the significance of a city set on a hill. Perhaps they instinctively thought of the city set on the hill as Jerusalem. It gave light because it was the centre of their faith. Jesus gave that fact a dramatic twist when he said that he – not Jerusalem – was the light of the world, and his disciples were to share in that mission.

[63]

Few things are more important for the Christian in this world than to realise the extent of its darkness. The problem with living in the darkness is the effect it has on one's ability to see clearly. It becomes difficult to distinguish one object from another. A person loses direction. He has lost his bearings. That is true morally, also. In the words of Jesus, 'If then the light within you is darkness, how great is that darkness!' (*Matt. 6:23*).

We live in such a world today. Men have lost their sense of moral bearings and are blind to the terrible consequences. We call evil good. We become morally confused. Some people who campaign against nuclear armaments because they are concerned for the future of humanity may also be those who are pro-abortion, and thus deny the future to millions of embryonic members of humanity. What logic is this? What enlightenment takes modern man back to practices that were abominated in what he describes with superior cynicism as 'the Dark Ages'?

How does this modern man spend his glorious life, now that he has escaped from the Christian faith? Curiously, although he has no time to read the Bible to investigate the faith he has rejected, he spends an average of four hours each day in devotion to a glass-fronted box! (How strange that this man who rejects Christian faith on 'modern' or 'philosophical' or 'scientific' grounds has not the slightest idea what that faith really is!)

Man is so completely surrounded by his moral darkness that he cannot see his moral and spiritual foolishness. If only he lived within a hundred miles of a city, it might light up his night sky, and he might see his profound spiritual need and repent! *You*, Jesus says, *are the city that man needs*.

This emphasis is further developed in the illustration of the lamp that is intended to give light to those who are in the house. The lamp is not to be hidden away. The Christian, who has become light in the Lord, should shine for his Lord. His holiness, or 'good deeds,' will then be seen, and others will be drawn to glorify God through his witness.

Peter echoes this thought when he says that we are a people chosen to declare the praises of him who called us out of our darkness into his marvellous light. Peter encourages us to 'live such good lives among the pagans that, though they accuse you of doing wrong, they may see your good deeds and glorify God on the day he visits us' (*I Pet. 2:12*).

The regeneration of men's lives is a sovereign work of God's grace. We cannot bring anyone to newness of life. But it is our responsibility to live the new life in order that others may be challenged by it. It is our responsibility to shine for Jesus Christ so that others will see his salvation expressed in the flesh-and-blood reality of our daily lives. This is the point Jesus is making: we have a responsibility to show the Christ-like life of light to those around us. We cannot hide it under a cover.

One final word should be said about Jesus' description of the role of the disciple in the world. It is generally agreed that Matthew's Gospel is, of all four Gospels, the most 'Jewish' in character. Yet, notice the sphere of the church's influence and witness. It is not restricted to the covenant community (the Jews). The disciples are to be the light of *the world*. They are not to hide or restrict the light of God, but to let it shine to all.

The implication is clear. Already in the Sermon on the Mount, Jesus is underlining the challenge which is stated so clearly in his Great Commission (*Matt. 28:18–20*): the whole world is to be our sphere of influence. To reduce it to anything less would be tantamount to restricting the power, authority, and grace of the Lord Jesus Christ. He has told us that the whole world is the sphere in which the gospel is to be proclaimed and lived out. All men are to hear it and see it.

Fulfilling this plan will demand that the whole of our lives be whole-heartedly and unceasingly devoted to him and to his service. That devotion will cost us everything. But surely those who are 'the light of the world' will give nothing less for him who is the light that the darkness can never overcome (*Jn. 1:5*).

Just what is involved in living in the light and in shining as the light of the world is further explained in Christ's searching words yet to come.

7

Jesus, the Law, and the Christian

MATTHEW 5

[17]*'Do not think that I have come to abolish the Law or the Prophets; I have not come to abolish them but to fulfil them.* [18]*I tell you the truth, until heaven and earth disappear, not the smallest letter, not the least stroke of a pen, will by any means disappear from the Law until everything is accomplished.* [19]*Anyone who breaks one of the least of these commandments and teaches others to do the same will be called least in the kingdom of heaven, but whoever practises and teaches these commands will be called great in the kingdom of heaven.* [20]*For I tell you that unless your righteousness surpasses that of the Pharisees and the teachers of the law, you will certainly not enter the kingdom of heaven.'*

*   *   *

John Newton, the converted slave trader and author of the hymn 'Amazing Grace,' was also an outstandingly wise correspondent with many of his contemporaries who sought his spiritual counsel. In one of his letters he wrote,

THE SERMON ON THE MOUNT

'Ignorance of the nature and design of the law is at the bottom of most of our religious mistakes.'[1] That is still true today. Perhaps more Christians are confused or uncertain about the role that God's law plays in their lives than about most things. That is why Jesus' words in Matthew 5:17–20 are so important. Here he explains to us the place the law should have in the Christian life.

What *is* the law? The first five books of the Old Testament are known collectively as 'the law' in distinction from 'the prophets' (see *Lk. 16:16*). More generally in Scripture, the words for law (*torah* in Hebrew, *nomos* in Greek) can mean a wide variety of things – commandment, principle, instruction, and so on. The meaning of the word *law*, therefore, can be determined only by examining its use in each context.

What, then, does *Jesus* mean when he speaks about the law in the course of the Sermon on the Mount? He uses the common distinction between the law and the prophets (*verse 17*). He also speaks about the law in terms of its commandments and commands (*verse 19*). Here he is referring particularly to the idea of the law as the specific commandments God has given to his people to regulate the whole of their lives – moral, religious, social, and political. What he goes on to say in 5:21–48 emphasises that when he speaks about the place of the law, he is thinking of *the commandments God gave to his people through the ministry of Moses*.

By this point in his sermon, Jesus has made it very clear what belonging to the kingdom of God means. What he has said is startling enough. But in some ways, what he has *not* said is even more startling. He has said nothing about the law and the importance of keeping it. He has said nothing about the traditional interpretations of the law, and the importance of observing them. No statement has

[1] *The Letters of John Newton*, Banner of Truth Trust, London, 1960, p.40.

[68]

issued from his lips encouraging reverence for the scribes and the Pharisees.

Did this mean that Jesus was overthrowing the law? He certainly was teaching that the way of salvation and entry into God's kingdom was not by merit gained through obedience to the law. Rather than feeling that they had achieved merit, Jesus' followers were poor in spirit, mourned for their sins, and received comfort and the kingdom of God. To the listening scribes and Pharisees, this must have sounded for all the world like the abolition of religion and of everything they stood for. So far, Jesus had said people could enter God's kingdom by God's grace; he had made not one single mention of the law!

The fear the Pharisees had has been shared by others since that day. Their concern was this: take away the law as the means of earning merit, and no one will make any effort to keep it. The law will lose its teeth, and no longer 'hold' people. They will live as they please, as the following ditty suggests:

> *Free from the law,*
> *O blessed condition!*
> *I can sin as I please,*
> *And still have remission.*

But nothing could be further from the teaching of Jesus, as the rest of his sermon shows. Christians are not antinomians, living morally loose lives. They hunger and thirst for righteousness, for a righteousness surpassing that of the Pharisees and teachers of the law (*5:20*).

Paul summarises the teaching of the gospel when he encounters the same objection Jesus faced to his teaching of salvation by grace: 'Do we, then, nullify the law by this faith? Not at all! Rather, we uphold the law' (*Rom. 3:31*). Later in Romans Paul expresses the same point even more fully when he tells us:

What the law was powerless to do in that it was weakened by the sinful nature, God did by sending his own Son in the likeness of sinful man to be a sin offering. And so he condemned sin in sinful man, in order that the righteous requirements of the law might be fully met in us, who do not live according to the sinful nature but according to the Spirit. (Rom. 8:3–4)

Jesus explains the place the law is to occupy in the kingdom of God by saying four things.

THE CONTINUING VALIDITY OF THE LAW

Jesus had not come to ignore or abolish the sacred Scriptures of the Old Testament. If only the Pharisees had listened to what he was saying, that fact would have been clear to them, for so much of his teaching in the Beatitudes employed the language and teaching of the Old Testament. Neither the law nor the prophets were put aside by his coming; rather, they were fulfilled (*5:17*).

Readers of Matthew's Gospel are already familiar with the way in which Jesus fulfils the prophets. The opening chapters are punctuated with the idea of fulfilment: 'All this took place to fulfil what the Lord had said through the prophet' (*Matt. 1:22; cf. 2:6, 15, 17, 23, 4:14*). But in what sense is the law fulfilled when we know that we are not justified before God by our efforts to keep it?

The law does three things. It expresses the character of God and his will for man's life. Further, it teaches us the true character of man. God's intention for man is that he live in accordance with the law of the Lord. Thirdly, the law teaches us the character of salvation.

If a life conformed to God's law is God's intention for man, then when we are restored to fellowship with him and live in his will (which is what salvation involves), we will begin to fulfil his intention. In Paul's words, the requirements of the law will be fulfilled in us as we walk according to the Spirit. Rather than contradict the gospel, the law of God, properly understood, goes hand in hand with it.

The Pharisees had not only failed to understand the gospel (to which they knew they were opposed); they also misunderstood the law (which they believed they upheld!).

Whatever else Jesus may have said about the law, he made it plain that he had not come to abolish it.

THE PRESENT FULFILMENT OF THE LAW

Christians are familiar with the idea that Jesus fulfils the prophecies of the Old Testament. As Paul says, 'No matter how many promises God has made, they are "Yes" in Christ' (*2 Cor. 1:20*). Jesus shows us what the promises of the Old Testament really meant. Until he came, God's people knew them and believed them, of course. But only when he fulfilled them were they able to say, 'Now I understand them.'

Jesus says the same is true of God's law. That point is often overlooked. In Matthew 5:17, Jesus is teaching that if we want to know what the law really means, we must look at him and what he does with it because he fulfils, or 'accomplishes,' the law (*5:18*). *How?*

Jesus fulfils the law in his doctrine, or teaching. He brings out the real significance of God's commands. The Pharisees accused Jesus of 'abolishing' the law. But, in fact, they were the ones who were abolishing it. Their traditional interpretations of the law weakened its power to search the motives of men's hearts. It was only in the exposition of Jesus (in Matthew 5:21–48, for example) that the real power of God's law could be felt. Jesus did not weaken the law. On the contrary, he let it out of the cage in which the Pharisees had imprisoned it, allowing it to pounce on our secret thoughts and motives, and tear to pieces our bland assumption that we are able to keep it in our own strength.

Jesus fulfils the law in his deeds and lifestyle. He shows the real meaning of the law.

We do not learn a great deal about the personal lives of the Pharisees from the Gospels, but we are left with the impression that they did not promote much joy among the people! Obedience to the law was, for them, a heavy task, and their ministries consequently placed heavy burdens on the shoulders of those who followed them. In Jesus' words, 'They tie up heavy loads and put them on men's shoulders, but they themselves are not willing to lift a finger to move them' (*Matt. 23:4*).

But the law of God was not a burden on Jesus' shoulders; rather, it was written in his heart. This is why the early church saw so clearly in Jesus the fulfilment of Psalm 40:8: 'To do your will, O my God, is my desire; your law is within my heart' (*cf. Heb. 10:7*). Jesus enjoyed doing God's will. It was 'meat and drink' to him: 'My food . . . is to do the will of him who sent me and to finish his work' (*Jn. 4:34*).

Jesus fulfils the law in his death. Jesus shows the reality of the law's holiness as he bears the penalty of breaking the law by taking our place before the judgment seat of God.

We often think that it is at Mount Sinai, where Moses received the Ten Commandments, that we learn how solemn any breach of the law is as we listen to the thunder and see the lightning flashes of God's holy presence. But it is really at the Cross alone that we discover the real meaning of the curse and judgement of God's broken covenant. There Jesus cried out, 'My God, I am forsaken. Why?' His cry of God-forsakenness, which pierced the darkness of the afternoon of his crucifixion, really says to us: 'This is the penalty of the broken law. This is the meaning of God's law. See how terrible its fulfilment is.'

But Jesus' death teaches us something else about the law. His death forms the prism that enables us to see the law in its component parts.

To the Old Testament believer, the law was the law. His whole life was bound by it. He did not pigeon-hole different parts of his life to be ruled by what we call the moral law, or the ceremonial law, or the civil law. There was no reason for him to do so because the state, the nation, or the church, were simply different ways of looking at the same thing. But that was no longer true after the death of Christ.

Jesus' death (and the Resurrection and Day of Pentecost which followed) marked a new era in God's dealings with his people. One of the chief elements in its 'newness' was its universal character. No longer were the church and the nation of Israel two ways of saying the same thing, or two different views of the same group of people.

In keeping with this, the New Testament writers recognised that by Jesus' death, certain elements in God's law had been fulfilled *in order to be abolished*. The ceremonies of the law – the daily, weekly, and yearly sacrifices – were abolished because their real meaning was to foreshadow the sacrifice that Christ himself would make. Since Christ had made one sacrifice for sin, valid for all time, no further sacrifices were required (*Heb. 10:11–18*). By necessity, therefore, the *ceremonial* element in the law was no longer binding on the church.

Of course this meant that the follower of Jesus saw something in the fulfilment of the law that an Old Testament believer would see only with great difficulty, if at all: part of the law given through Moses was to last only until Christ came. As a consequence, the early church

[73]

gradually came to see that Jesus had abolished the ritual teaching of the Old Testament on 'clean' and 'unclean' animals and food. (See *Acts 11:4–10*, then *Mark 7:19* and *Romans 14:14*).

But our Lord's death also unveiled another element in the law: there were aspects of it that applied to the nation of Israel but were no longer relevant to the church as the people of God. The church was not governed by the same civil code that governed the people of Israel. It is clear that the early church did not regard it as its responsibility to stone to death stubborn children or those who committed adultery. Now the church was to 'hand over to Satan' such people, 'so that the sinful nature may be destroyed, and his [the sinner's] spirit saved on the day of the Lord' (*1 Cor. 5:5; cf. 1 Tim. 1:20*).

Jesus fulfils the law in his disciples. Jesus fulfils the law by writing it in the hearts of his disciples, through the ministry of his Spirit. This lies at the heart of the promise of the new covenant: 'This is the covenant I will make with the house of Israel after that time. . . . I will put my law in their minds and write it on their hearts' (*Jer. 31:33*). As we walk by the Spirit, we fulfil the desires of the Spirit, not the desires of the flesh (*Gal. 5:16*). We do what the law requires (*Rom. 8:3–4*), and delight to do so.

God's law is no longer an external rule that we find burdensome. Because God has given us a new heart committed to him and his ways, we want to obey him. That is often one of the first discoveries a new Christian makes. Whereas before he struggled against God's law, now he finds that he has a heart to obey it. So, in his followers, Jesus begins to show the law's meaning, too.

It is a great mistake, then, to think that Jesus abolished the commandments and taught us that 'all we need is love.' For love *means* fulfilling the law (*Rom. 13:10*). In fact, in the New Testament it is John, the 'apostle of love,' who underlines the important place of the law for the believer. To show that love and law harmonise in the Christian life, he frequently echoes Jesus' words, 'If you love me you will obey what I command' (*Jn. 14:15*) and, 'If you obey my commands you will abide in my love' (*Jn. 15:10.*). We know that we have come to know God if we obey his commands (*1 Jn. 2:3*). Those who keep his commands live in him, and he lives in them (*1 Jn. 3:24*). Love for God means keeping his commands (*1 Jn. 5:3*).

In this respect, the Christian life is like one of the mighty steam engines of the railways of the past, the kind on which Casey Jones used to go 'a steamin' and a rollin'!' They needed fuel for the fire for power. But they also needed tracks, to direct their energy. Love for Christ, in the power of the Spirit, is the energy of the Christian life. But that love needs tracks on which to run if it is ever to get to its intended destination.

God's law provides us with those tracks. That is why many places in the New Testament allude to the teaching of Exodus 20 (the giving of the Ten Commandments through Moses). These commandments are the sacred way in which we are to walk. Rather than restrict us, these tracks give us freedom to move in a Godward direction.

THE DEEP SPIRITUALITY OF THE LAW

Some of those people listening to Jesus preach the Sermon on the Mount simply assumed that he was lowering God's standard of morality. Perhaps others hoped that he was! Then he said something that must have sounded devastating to them all: 'I tell you that unless your righteousness surpasses that of the Pharisees and the teachers of the law, you will certainly not enter the kingdom of heaven' (*5:20*).

[75]

This was a staggering statement. After all, it was said that 'if only two men are allowed to enter Heaven, then one will certainly be a teacher of the law and the other a Pharisee.' There might be a problem in saying who was superior, but certainly no one else was even considered as a candidate! With some 248 regulations and 365 prohibitions to deal with, salvation was certainly for the professionals! Only the righteousness of a scribe or a Pharisee, it was assumed, would make the grade.

What did Jesus mean? It has sometimes been assumed he meant something like this. The righteousness that the Pharisee possesses will not gain him entrance into the kingdom of heaven. Only God's gift of righteousness to man will do that (*cf. Rom. 1:16–17*). That is, no doubt, Jesus' meaning, but its implications are not always fully understood. Jesus Christ not only justifies us by sharing with us his righteousness; he also sanctifies and transforms us by making us righteous. In other words, our righteousness really must surpass that of the Pharisees. For if we are not more righteous than they are, we are not righteous at all.

The verses that follow (*5:21–48*) illustrate what Jesus meant. Pharisaic righteousness was skin deep; Christian righteousness is to be real. It is to be true heart conformity to the law of God. Our obedience to the law is not to be merely external and ceremonial, but real and spiritual. Our understanding of it is not merely traditional and superficial (cleansing the outside of the cup, but not the inside of the heart [*Matt. 23:25*]).

This is the practical fulfilment of the law that marks Jesus' disciples. They understand that the law is spiritual (*Rom. 7:14*). They respond to it, not in their own strength, but in the power of the Spirit, who cleanses and renews their hearts.

THE DISTINGUISHING FUNCTION OF THE LAW

Jesus said: 'Anyone who breaks one of the least of these commandments and teaches others to do the same will be called least in the kingdom of heaven, but whoever practises and teaches these commands will be called great in the kingdom of heaven' (*5:19*).

With these words, is Jesus reversing his earlier teaching that we enter the kingdom of God through grace? Surely not. Rather, he is saying that our attitude to the law of God is an index of our attitude to God himself. If we treat the law lightly and encourage others to do so (if we have a settled and consistent attitude of antagonism toward it), we show that we are strangers to the promise of the new covenant in Christ. But if we love and keep even the least of the Lord's commandments, and we encourage others to do so as well (if we have a settled attitude of obedience), that is a sure mark that we love Christ and belong to his kingdom.

The law is not the basis on which we merit salvation, but it does provide a test to distinguish between those who belong to the kingdom of salvation and those who are outside of it. It is the real test of whether we have been 'born again' or not. If we have been, then God's law has been written in our hearts, and we obey it joyfully. If we have not been, we may make a pretence at living the new life, but eventually the mask will be dropped, and we will despise some of God's laws (perhaps what Jesus calls 'the least of these commandments'). Soon we will encourage others to do so as well. And thus we will be barred from the kingdom of heaven.

Sin is lawlessness, says John (*1 Jn. 3:4*). But the Christian has turned away from sin, to a life of cleanliness. That is why the apostle Paul asks, 'Do we, then, nullify the law by this faith? Not at all! Rather, we uphold the law' (*Rom. 3:31*).

8
The Pure
in Heart

MATTHEW 5

²¹*'You have heard that it was said to the people long ago, "Do not murder, and anyone who murders will be subject to judgment."* ²²*But I tell you that anyone who is angry with his brother will be subject to judgment. Again, anyone who says to his brother, "Raca," is answerable to the Sanhedrin. But anyone who says, "You fool!" will be in danger of the fire of hell.*

²³*'Therefore, if you are offering your gift at the altar and there remember that your brother has something against you,* ²⁴*leave your gift there in front of the altar. First go and be reconciled to your brother; then come and offer your gift.*

²⁵*'Settle matters quickly with your adversary who is taking you to court. Do it while you are still with him on the way, or he may hand you over to the judge, and the judge may hand you over to the officer, and you may be thrown into prison.* ²⁶*I tell you the truth, you will not get out until you have paid the last penny.*

²⁷*'You have heard that it was said, "Do not commit adultery."* ²⁸*But I tell you that anyone who looks at a woman*

*lustfully has already committed adultery with her in his heart.*²⁹*If your right eye causes you to sin, gouge it out and throw it away. It is better for you to lose one part of your body than for your whole body to be thrown into hell.*³⁰*And if your right hand causes you to sin, cut it off and throw it away. It is better for you to lose one part of your body than for your whole body to go into hell.*

³¹*'It has been said, "Anyone who divorces his wife must give her a certificate of divorce."* ³²*But I tell you that anyone who divorces his wife, except for marital unfaithfulness, causes her to commit adultery, and anyone who marries a woman so divorced commits adultery.'*

★ ★ ★

Jesus came to fulfil the law, not to destroy it. In fact, as we have seen, Jesus teaches that the law of God is an essential diagnostic tool. Whether we break it or keep it, and whether we encourage others to break it or keep it, is an indication of our true spiritual condition. It is the standard for evaluation in the kingdom of God (*Matt. 5:19*), but not the standard for entrance into the kingdom. Rather than dispensing with righteousness, Jesus tell his disciples that unless their righteousness surpasses that of the Pharisees and the teachers of the law, they will certainly not enter the kingdom of heaven.

What, then, are we to make of the statements that follow in Matthew 5:21–48? They share the same basic format, in which a contrast is drawn between what was 'said to the people long ago' and what 'I [Jesus] tell you' (*Matt. 5:21–22; 27–28; 31–32; 33–34; 38–39; 43–44*).

At first, it may seem that Jesus is contradicting the teaching of the Old Testament law. Many of the things that he tells us were 'said to the people long ago' seem to be direct quotations from the pages of the Old Testament. This has sometimes led students to the conclusion that

Jesus is dispensing with the Old Testament teachings, and introducing a new dimension of faith altogether – a faith of the heart that is inward rather than outward, gracious rather than legal. After all, does John not say, 'The *law* was given through *Moses; grace and truth* came through *Jesus Christ*' (*Jn. 1:17*)?

However, to contrast the teaching of Jesus with the law in this way is a mistake. It does injustice to what Jesus actually says in these verses, and it does a grave injustice to the law of God. These points are so important that it is worth spending time thinking them through, for understanding the place of the law in the Christian life is one of the most crucial issues for contemporary disciples.

Why does this *contrast*, even *contradiction*, between the teaching of Jesus and that of the law do such disservice to the law? It suggests that the law (and for that matter, Old Testament religion) was merely external. But we need only to read some of the psalms to see how far this is from the truth. God's people loved his law; they realised that it spoke to the heart. It was not merely an external code, but penetrated to the innermost recesses of their being and searched out their secret thoughts and plans (*see Ps. 19:7–14 and 119:70–72*). As we read Jesus' exposition, and the reflections of Old Testament believers on the law, we see that there is no contradiction.

To suggest such a contradiction also misses the point that Jesus is making. He is not dispensing with the law, or contradicting it. He could not be doing that, for a number of important reasons.

1. Jesus has just said that he did not come to abolish the law, but to fulfil it. He stressed that not a jot or tittle would disappear until it was fulfilled. Were he to overthrow the teaching of the law in the verses that follow, he would do more than that; he would overthrow his own teaching.

2. The basic contrast in these verses is not only between the things that are said, but between the people who say them. Jesus contrasts what has been said by *others* with what *he* says. His words are quite emphatic: 'But *I* say.' He uses both the first person singular of the verb – *legō* – 'I say,' and the first person singular pronoun – *egō* – 'I, for emphasis. We might say, '*I myself say*.' The issue at stake here is one of authority, not merely one of content.

3. But still more important is the fact that the words *said to the people long ago* are not necessarily quotations from Scripture. Some of them are, but there are also additions to Scripture, and in one case there is a contradiction of Scripture: We are to love our neighbour (*Lev. 19:18*), but the Old Testament did not give a general command to God's people to 'hate your enemy' (*Matt. 5:43*). This suggests very clearly that Jesus is not placing his own teaching directly against that of the Old Testament.

4. As a matter of fact, Jesus does not give us a series of contradictions. Rather than dispense with the law of God, it is clear from his searching teaching that he is giving a thorough, heart-searching exposition of it.

5. The real contrast in this section is between the meaning of the law *according to Jesus* and the meaning of the law *according to religious tradition and the ancient teachers*. It may be that the words *to the people long ago* should be translated '*by* the people long ago,' that is, the religious teachers, not the authors of Scripture.

It is clear that Jesus introduces these various statements with a phrase that differs from his usual introduction to biblical quotations. He does not say, 'It is written,' but, 'It was said.' In view of his emphasis on the written nature of the law of God in verse 18 (where he speaks of letters and strokes of the pen), Jesus is not referring here to texts in Scripture, but to the traditional teaching of the rabbis.

s.o.m.—7

It is no accident that these contrasts are set in the context of Jesus as the fulfilment of the Exodus: he is the Son God has called out of Egypt (*Matt. 2:15*); he passes through the waters in his baptism (*Matt. 3:13–17*); he is tested in the wilderness (*Matt. 4:1–11*); he expounds the law of God in the mountainous region (*Matt. 5:1*). Rather than displace the teaching God had given through Moses, Jesus' whole ministry is identified by Matthew as the fulfilment of God's teaching.

If, then, Jesus is to be heard here as the True Teacher of God's word, what is his teaching? In the rest of this chapter, we will look at the first three elements in our Lord's exposition.

MURDER WITHOUT KNIVES

The law forbids murder. But it was characteristic of the theologians then (as now!) to ask, 'Exactly what does this mean? When is murder really murder?' The discussions and distinctions had the inevitable result of narrowing down the act of murder to certain situations and conditions.

Jesus points out that by doing this, the full force of God's word is destroyed. Jesus explains that the commandment not only forbids the outward act but also every thought and word that seeks to destroy a man's life. Moreover, like every other command, by forbidding an activity, Jesus is teaching that we should take every possible step to promote the opposite. In this case, instead of murdering by hand or mouth, we should seek with all our powers to have right relationships with all of our brothers.

For Jesus, to kill with a knife, or to engage in character assassination through anger, or to belittle another by calling him 'fool' is part and parcel of the same spiritual sickness. Clearly, he does not mean that it makes no difference whether we gossip or stab, but he does mean that both activities reveal the same animosity of heart to our neighbours.

There *are* times when men are fools. Jesus said so himself (*Matt. 23:17; Lk. 12:20*). And Scripture teaches us to recognise that (*Ps. 14:1; 49:10; Prov. 1:7,22,32*). Jesus does not have that stubborn rebellion against God in mind here, but the deliberate belittling of someone's person because of the animosity and hatred of our own heart, and the desire to have mastery over them. That is murder.

It is not only in the sordid muckraking of some elements of the media that such public assassination takes place. It is not unknown among professing Christians. Men build empires in the church as well as in the world, and will brook no rival. In the spirit of the Pharisees, they wrongly assume that they can retain clean hands by ruining someone's reputation with a word, under the cover of 'getting at the truth.'

How very careful we need to be with our spirits and the tongues that give expression to them! No wonder the New Testament gives clear teaching about controlling what we say (*Matt. 12:34; 15:18; Eph. 4:29; Jas. 3:1-12*). Our words are the index of our true spiritual condition.

Jesus recognised that we cannot be trusted in our judgement of the seriousness of careless speech. We treat the damage we do with our lips very lightly because we do not see the corpses we leave behind. That is why Jesus invades our moral slumber by telling us how serious this is in the sight of God. He uses language we readily understand: anger incurs judgment; using terms of contempt (like *raca*) is worthy of condemnation by the highest court (*5:22*); calling someone a fool fits us for hell.

Jesus is probably not placing these sins on a scale of seriousness in the kingdom of God; he is simply stressing vividly that *they are far more serious than most of us assume*. In fact, our insensitivity to their real seriousness is indicative of the dullness of our spiritual senses.

In the verses that follow (*23–26*), the *necessity* and *urgency* of reconciliation in place of animosity are stressed by two illustrations. Here Jesus is showing us that when an activity is forbidden in God's word, its positive counterpart is commanded. If we are *not* to engage in physical or verbal murder, we *are* to engage in personal reconciliation.

Picture a man in church. He is about to express his devotion to the Lord in worship and in his offering. But he has not been enjoying fellowship with his brother. There is disharmony in the relationship. Jesus says the man should leave his offering, be reconciled to his brother, and then return to worship God with a clear conscience and full heart.

Is Jesus saying that the only important thing in worship is right relationships with our fellow men? Hardly! He recognises that our relationship with God is primary, but we always appear before God as those who are related, rightly or wrongly, to our fellow men. What we are before God involves how we are related to others. And if we are at enmity with others, how can we come into the Lord's presence with clean hands and a pure heart? It is monstrous to think that he will find our hypocritical offering acceptable.

Obedience is better than sacrifice (*1 Sam. 15:22*). As Peter shows, this principle extends to the home and family: husbands are to treat their wives with respect and as heirs of the gracious gift of life *so that nothing will hinder their prayers* (*1 Pet. 3:7*). The principle is clear: right relationships with others are part of the meaning of the commandment not to murder. They are essential if our righteousness is to go down deeper than that of the scribes and Pharisees.

Jesus gives us another illustration. Two men are on their way to court to settle a dispute between them. They are still arguing on the way! Jesus says the two men should settle the matter *now*, before they are in the courtroom with the judge. It may be costly to settle it now; it will certainly be humbling. But if it continues, one man may find himself in prison and unable to get out until he has paid the last penny (*5:26*).

Reading these verses *in their context* safeguards us from confusion in understanding what Jesus is saying. These two examples are not pieces of advice, or laws, either for church behaviour or for solving legal problems! They are, rather, illustrations of how vital it is to have right relationships with others. The illustration of the man in church underlines the necessity of reconciliation. The illustration of two men going to court underlines the urgency of reconciliation.

Animosity is a time bomb; we do not know when it will 'go off.' We must deal with it quickly, before the consequences of our bitterness get completely out of control. Most human relationships that are destroyed could have been preserved if there had been communication and action *at the right time*. Jesus says that the right time is as soon as we are conscious that we are at enmity with our brother (*Matt. 5:23*).

One further point should be noted from this section. Jesus urges us to seek reconciliation when 'your brother has something against you' (*5:23*), or when 'your adversary . . . is taking you to court' (*5:25*). Jesus is telling us that we should, as far as possible, remove all basis for enmity. But he is not urging us to share every thought in our hearts during the process of reconciliation. Our secret thoughts and sins will not be sanctified by telling others about them. Doing so has led many Christians (and those they have spoken to) into unhappy and sometimes disastrous situations. Jesus is not telling us to 'hang out our dirty linen in public,' but rather to deal urgently and fully with all breakdowns in fellowship before they lead to spiritual assassination.

ADULTERY IN THE HEART

The law of God forbids all adultery (*Ex. 20:14*). The Old Testament penalty was death (*Lev. 20:10*). But for all practical purposes, the scribes reduced this law to, 'You shall not be found guilty of committing adultery.' In some cases they virtually dispensed with the temptation to commit adultery by making divorce possible on the most trivial of grounds. Deuteronomy 24:1 required a man whose wife 'becomes displeasing to him because he finds something *indecent* about her' to give a certificate of divorce to her. According to some of the scribes, a man could divorce his wife if he grew 'cool' toward her or if he did not like her cooking. A law that was clearly intended to safeguard the women in Israel was turned into an escape clause for self-indulgent men.

Jesus calls a halt to all such distorting of God's word. He lets it speak with full force. The lust that leads to adultery will also lead a man to hell. Better to deal with the lust now – to deny oneself now – than to live with eternal self-recrimination. Far from simply forbidding *some* acts of immorality, Jesus says God's law demands purity and integrity in our hearts and in our thoughts about others.

We stressed earlier that understanding God's law is a critical issue for Christians today. Verses 27–30 illustrate the point vividly. Sexual relations have become the door through which many professing Christians have walked to their destruction. Perhaps evangelicals have rather naïvely assumed that the drift in secular morality 'could never happen to us.' But it has, and already our magazines and pastoral journals abound with discussions on this very issue.

Jesus does not make such naïve assumptions. He knows what is in all men's hearts (*Jn. 2:25*). He recognises that no man is free from temptation, nor is any man free (in this life at least) from the influence of indwelling sin.

Jesus speaks about adultery, but it is clear from his exposition that he has *any* sexual immorality in view. He stresses that its root is to be found in the heart. The man who *looks* at a woman *lustfully* commits heart adultery with her.

God made men and women to be attracted to each other, to need each other, and to enter into relationships with each other that have physical, spiritual, and mental dimensions. We have, by God's goodness, the ability to share in the reproduction of other human beings, in a context of the closest imaginable human relationship – both physically and spiritually. The gift of sexual relationship is unequivocally good. It is God's gift.

But the supreme reason for that gift is *companionship*. God brought Eve to Adam in the Garden of Eden because it was 'not good for the man to be alone' (*Gen. 2:18*). It is within that bond of committed fellowship that family life is to be established, and our sexual instincts are to find their fulfilment.

In order to become one flesh, 'a man will leave his father and mother and be united to his wife' (*Gen. 2:24*). At the heart of the relationship lies the element of *commitment* – leaving parents and uniting with one's wife or husband. This is God's order, and we breach it at our own peril and at the risk of destroying our society.

The commandment against adultery is set in this context. Adultery actually involves the breach of several of God's commandments. It involves disobedience of the specific command that forbids it. Therefore, it involves disobedience of the Lord whom we are to worship. It involves theft – another person's companion – as a result of coveting what belongs to another. Far from being exciting as a lifestyle, its pleasure is that of theft and idolatry. It is an ugly and base act, and would be seen as such were the scales that blind us torn from our eyes and the foolishness that desensitises us cleansed from our heart.

This is why adultery is so serious. It shatters people's lives, disrupts families and despises God. It was therefore considered worthy of the death sentence in the Old Testament (*Lev. 20:10*). Such a sentence was intended to awaken God's people to the deadly nature of immorality. Few things bring more pain to more people in today's society.

How, then, can we live in our society and remain faithful to the Lord's word? Jesus tells us that we must guard our hearts if we are to do so.

Clearly, our appreciation of men and women – their looks, their gifts, their graces – cannot be wrong. Jesus is not forbidding *looking*, but *lusting looks*. He is telling us that when we recognise our tendency to sin, we must commit ourselves to staying within the boundaries that God has set around us. We must guard our heart and our actions – gestures and looks – within those boundary lines.

If we are men, then, like Job, we will say, 'I made a covenant with my eyes not to look lustfully at a girl' (*Job 31:1*). If we are women, we will make a similar covenant with the Lord. We will not play with our own emotions, and we will be scrupulous not to do so with the emotions of others. We will vow to treat other Christians as brothers and sisters in complete purity (see *1 Tim. 5:2*). Only as we are brought by God into the context of commitment to another, will we be prepared to share what is appropriate only for the marriage relationship.

We may react to this teaching in various ways. Some regard it as the end of all fun and excitement in life. This restraint sounds so sober and serious – what of the joy the Christian life is supposed to exhibit? That is precisely the point. Jesus recognised that sinners could never know true and lasting joy as long as they indulged themselves. True joy, resurrection joy, always lies for the Christian on the other side of sharing in Jesus' death to sin. That is as applicable to sexual purity as to anything else.

Furthermore, sexual infidelity is a sure way to ruin marital joy, whether it takes place before or during marriage. It either hardens our heart and blights a truly Christian marriage, or it sears our conscience and creates a guilt that *God* may indeed forgive, but that *we* will probably never be able to forget. Worst of all, Jesus says, it may be the first stepping stone leading to the crossroads of our whole spiritual pilgrimage. Sexual immorality (like any other sin) makes repentance far more difficult. Inability to repent led Esau and Judas to destruction (*Heb. 12:17*). Beware the deceitfulness of a momentary gratification that will lead to life-long recrimination.

How, then, can we keep our way pure? Jesus' vivid illustrations suggest a number of important general principles. 1. Realise where yielding to sinful lusts will lead you. Jesus says that hell is the direction in which all sin leads (*Matt. 5:29–30*). Fix that in your mind.

2. Deal with the real cause of your sin. If it is the right eye that causes you to sin, says Jesus, gouge it out. Could we substitute something else? No, says Jesus.

Most of us know what he means. We offer God substitutes. If we can hold on to our favourite lust, we are

[89]

prepared to sacrifice other things. We will do more Bible reading, attend times of prayer, give more sacrificially. We may even be prepared to give far more to the Lord's work – anything except give up our 'right eye.' But failure to 'gouge it out' cannot be remedied by substitute offerings of obedience or sacrifice.

3. Act decisively, immediately, even if it must be painful. Jesus gives a horrific description of what other New Testament writers call 'mortification.' It is like gouging out your eye or cutting off a limb. There will be pain, tears, blood. There will be 'withdrawal symptoms' after the amputation. The consequences seem almost unbearable. But the drastic nature of the remedy is simply the index of the radical danger of the sin. It is not a situation for negotiation. Obedience cannot be negotiated, nor can heaven and hell.

4. Realise especially that your lust is not the whole of your life, and weigh against its influence all that will be yours by abandoning it. It is better to lose your eye and keep your body than to lose all in hell, Jesus states.

What happens when we are caught up in some specific sin? We become the objects of blackmail. We think, or Satan says, 'If you deal with this sin as Jesus says, what will be left for you? Think of the long road back to spiritual recovery. Think of what you will lose if you say no.' Such is the nature of the attraction and bondage of sin that it becomes all-consuming. It demands all we can give.

But Jesus gives us the hope of a new perspective. Gouge out the offending eye, but save your life. Yes, you may have committed sin the memory of which you will never be able to erase, even though it be forgiven. But you will have taken steps on the way to life and turned away from the doorway to death. Do not be deceived into a hopeless abandonment to sin.

DIVORCE

We have seen that the word of God had been distorted by
religious traditions. The passage that was intended to
regulate man's rebellion against God's purpose in marriage was distorted to provide an excuse for divorce. The
hard hearts that this law was meant to restrain used it to
their own ends.

Jesus confirms that God hates divorce (*Mal. 2:16*). Only
one exception is made in this passage: the marital
unfaithfulness of one spouse. The word Matthew uses is
porneia. By the time this Gospel was written, the word
carried the fairly wide meaning of sexual immorality and
unfaithfulness.

In any other case, divorce 'makes' the woman commit
adultery, and anyone who then marries a divorced woman
commits adultery. Jesus has in view the fact that in his
society the divorced woman might be driven to remarry
for the sake of her own sustenance. Only in the case of
adultery would such a remarriage not be an act of adultery
itself.

Why is this? The explanation lies in the Old Testament
law. The penalty for adultery in Jewish law was death
(*Lev. 20:10*). Obviously, when this penalty was exacted,
the marriage came to an abrupt end, and the living partner
was free to marry again.

In Jesus' time (when Palestine was under Roman
occupation), this death penalty was not carried out. The
person who committed adultery lived. But Jesus' teaching
seems to suggest *the rightness of acting as if the penalty had
been carried out*. In this case, the wronged partner would
be free to marry again. There was no contradiction of the
Old Testament law in this.

Throughout the ages, Christians have differed on the
significance of these words in Matthew 5:31–32. It is wise,

therefore, to assess their teaching point by point, indicating what seems to be clear, and what deductions Christians have drawn from them.

1. Scripture clearly teaches, and this passage certainly underscores, that God's design is permanent commitment in marriage. The destruction of a marriage is carnage in God's sight.

2. This passage provides us with Jesus' corrective for divorce-on-demand, the consequences of which are disastrous for the lives of whole families.

3. This passage emphasises that divorce on unbiblical grounds complicates sin rather than cures it, and may implicate others in sin rather than absolve them.

There is wide agreement on these three points. Many Christians (this writer included) would add two further points, which are also made in the *Westminster Confession of Faith*.

4. Jesus recognises that Scripture itself taught that sexual immorality can destroy marriage bonds. In the Old Testament, sexual sin was regulated by the death penalty setting the other partner free from the marriage. Although that penalty is no longer used, its *effect* is still relevant.

5. In view of this Old Testament background, in which the marriage ceased to be, so in the New Testament era, someone who is divorced following such marital infidelity can act as though the other partner has ceased to be, and can remarry.

But concluding all this, we must write, with great sadness, the words of our Lord himself:

> *Moses permitted you to divorce your wives because your hearts were hard. But it was not this way from the beginning. I tell you that anyone who divorces his wife, except for marital unfaithfulness, and marries another woman commits adultery.* (Matt. 19:8–9)

How, then, can we maintain marital faithfulness? Jesus does not expand on this in 5:31–32, but his answer can be found in the previous section of the sermon (*5:27–30*).

Marriage is a covenant (see *Prov. 2:17* and *Mal. 2:14*). We enter into it as a lifelong promise 'to have and to hold from this day forward; for better, for worse; for richer, for poorer; in sickness and in health, *until God shall separate us by death.*' Failure to keep that covenant is to live a lie before God and man. Bind it, therefore, on your heart. Decide that nothing will breach it. Strengthen it by genuinely 'having and holding' your partner, loving and cherishing them by God's grace. And gouge out from your heart anything that might destroy the joy of your relationship.

It is better, says Jesus, to lose a moment, a day, a week, a month, a year, of stolen pleasure than to lose all – self, wife, family, grace – and finally be cast into hell for despising the word of the Lord.

Who can read such teaching without trembling? May God help us to be faithful – to our spouse (if we are married), for our spouse (if we are to be married in the future) – or simply to God himself (if we remain single).

9
Oaths, Eyes, and Enemies

33'*Again, you have heard that it was said to the people long ago,
"Do not break your oath, but keep the oaths you have made to the
Lord." *34But I tell you, Do not swear at all: either by heaven,
for it is God's throne; *35or by the earth, for it is his footstool; or by
Jerusalem, for it is the city of the Great King. *36And do not
swear by your head, for you cannot make even one hair white or
black. *37Simply let your "Yes" be "Yes", and your "No,"
"No"; anything beyond this comes from the evil one.*

*38'You have heard that it was said, "Eye for eye, and tooth
for tooth." *39But I tell you, Do not resist an evil person. If
someone strikes you on the right cheek, turn to him the other also.
*40And if someone wants to sue you and take your tunic, let him
have your cloak as well. *41If someone forces you to go one mile,
go with him two miles. *42Give to the one who asks you, and do
not turn away from the one who wants to borrow from you.*

*43'You have heard that it was said, "Love your neighbour
and hate your enemy." *44But I tell you, Love your enemies and
pray for those who persecute you, *45that you may be sons of your
Father in heaven. He causes his sun to rise on the evil and the*

good, and sends rain on the righteous and the unrighteous. ⁴⁶*If you love those who love you, what reward will you get? Are not even the tax collectors doing that?* ⁴⁷*And if you greet only your brothers, what are you doing more than others? Do not even pagans do that?* ⁴⁸*Be perfect, therefore, as your heavenly Father is perfect.'*

★   ★   ★

As a teacher without parallel, our Lord draws out the real significance of the Old Testament law, just as he would later draw out more clearly the significance of the Old Testament prophets (*see Lk. 24:25–27, 44–47*). We have seen that his principle to fulfil, not to destroy the law is already expressed in the antithesis he draws in Matthew 5:21–32. Rather than play down its teaching, he has shown how searching and probing it really is. What at first appears to be a contrast is really Jesus' proper explanation and application.

The illustrations of Jesus' teaching seem to be divided into two groups of three, the second triad introduced by the word *again* in verse 33. The division is not based on any clearcut difference in content; indeed, it may simply break up the material for learning purposes. (The whole Sermon on the Mount bears indications that it was intended for memorisation.) In verses 33–48, Jesus deals with the swearing of oaths, the question of retaliation, and our attitude to our enemies. In each of these areas, as we shall see, he demonstrates how the Christian is 'different,' even 'extraordinary' (*v. 47*).

SAY 'YES' OR 'NO'

The taking of oaths and vows was part of life for Jesus' contemporaries. The two kinds of promises were distinct.

An *oath* was concerned with one's future actions. A *vow* was related to objects and their use. Sometimes the effect was one and the same. According to the Old Testament, in swearing an oath, the Lord's name was not to be used falsely (*Lev. 19:12*). On this basis, the Jews developed a 'theology of oaths.'

Jesus seems to sweep all this aside by saying, 'Do not swear at all' (*Matt. 5:34*). At first glance, this seems to be a simple and direct prohibition of oath-taking. Many Christians have held that view, and some still do. On grounds of conscience and obedience to their understanding of the commands of Jesus, they will refuse to take an oath in a court of law.

It is highly unlikely that this is what Jesus intended. Later in his ministry, he was obviously prepared to speak under oath during his trial: 'The high priest said to him, "I charge you under oath by the living God: Tell us if you are the Christ, the Son of God." "Yes, it is as you say," Jesus replied' (*Matt. 26:63-64*). When he was under oath, Jesus broke the silence he had maintained in the earlier part of the proceedings (*Matt. 26:63*), as though recognising the binding nature of being put under oath.

In fact, the issue that Jesus is raising is far more widely applicable than the question of taking an oath in court. The context in which he is speaking underlines this.

Jesus forbids swearing by heaven, earth, Jerusalem, and one's own head (*5:34–36*). Why would anyone do that in the first place? People were swearing oaths by these things without using God's name, and on that basis releasing themselves from fulfilling the promise they had given. 'Of course,' they would argue, 'had I sworn by God's name to keep my oath, I would have fulfilled it. But the fact that I swore by the earth indicates that my commitment was not an absolute one.' Jesus says two things about this.

It is utter hypocrisy. Heaven is God's throne, earth his footstool, Jerusalem his city, and he numbers the hairs of our heads and chooses their colour. That being so, *no promise can ever be made, no word ever spoken, without it being done in the presence of God.*

It is deep-seated dishonesty. What masquerades as theology is rank untruth. To swear by these things is to give the appearance of serious commitment. It is to suggest that one's word is one's bond, when all the time, behind the sign of integrity, one's heart is full of duplicity. Jesus abhors such a lack of moral integrity and seriousness.

How, then, is the Christian to live? Why should he not swear at all? He should let his 'yes' *mean* 'yes,' and his 'no' *mean* 'no.' He does not need to call on God to witness what he says because God is watching him and is present as he speaks, knowing his heart through and through. Anything beyond this straightforward honesty in our speech comes, says Jesus, 'from the evil one.'

Have you ever listened to one of those amusing conversations children have, when one asks a question that the other does not really answer? It may go like this:

'Did you take my biscuit?'

'I was watching television.'

'I didn't ask whether you were watching television. I asked if you took my biscuit.'

'There's another one in the box.'

'Did you take *my* biscuit? *Answer yes or no!*'

Jesus wants our answers to be straight-forward 'yes' or 'no' – without duplicity and without embellishment. *Truth is sacred*, and our speech should honour it.

Have we lost this value today in the Christian life as much as we fear it has been lost in public life? Is our 'yes' really 'yes'? Does it carry definite commitment? Or are we given to modifying the truth and disguising it? Is our word reliable? Do we do what we say we will do? Can people trust us as models of integrity? These are the very practical, day-to-day issues that Jesus raises here.

Jesus shows us what will introduce and maintain such integrity in our speech. We are always in the presence of God. He sees us and hears us. Every promise we give, every word we speak, we do before his face.

Would you live in full view of God's face, and live a lie in his presence?

TURN THE OTHER CHEEK

Of the entire Sermon on the Mount, no ideas are more frequently alluded to than the ones that follow: an eye for an eye; turn the other cheek; go the extra mile. They are still colourful expressions in the English language. For some people, they are the essence of Christianity. These statements have been used to explain and justify pacifism, by Christians and by others. For the great Russian author Leo Tolstoy (who consequently had a major influence on Mahatma Ghandi), these words produced a revolutionary effect. But what do they mean?

It is always an important principle in Bible study to remember the context in which a passage appears. If we do not 'hear' it in proper context, we might decide it means something quite different from what the speaker or author intended.

I recall saying to a colleague one day, 'The spirit is willing, but the flesh is weak.' He told me of a computer programme designed to translate English statements into Russian. This very statement had been fed into the computer. The resulting Russian version translated back into English as 'The whisky is stronger than the beef'! Clearly, the computer programme had not 'heard' the context of the statement.

The same danger often exists when we listen to Scripture without keeping the context in mind.

The context of Jesus' words is, we have seen, his exposition of the real meaning of the law of God. That law included the principle of 'an eye for an eye' (*Deut. 19:21*). If Jesus is following the pattern of the previous elements in his teaching, we would expect that he would go on to explain the real *purpose* that lay behind this law. First, we should see whether this is what he does.

What was the purpose of this law, and the justice that it expressed? Clearly, it was to limit and, if necessary, restrain retaliation. It seems, however, that this law was used as the justification for gaining even limited retaliation and revenge. That was to misunderstand the purpose of the law. Since it was meant to restrain personal vindictiveness and retaliation, the real fulfilment of it would be found in the man who did not seek such revenge. In the same way, the real fulfilment of the law about divorce was not found in stretching the law about divorce to its limit, but in faithful, lifelong marriage.

When Jesus speaks of the children of his kingdom not resisting one who is evil, the background for what he says is a legal one. In fact, the word *resist* in verse 39 is an explicitly legal term and might be translated, 'take to court' or 'give testimony against.' Jesus is expounding the desire of God in this way: do not stand on your legal rights as Christians, and bleed this law and others for all they are worth.

Behind this lies the principle by which every Christian is called to live: do not make your 'rights' the basis for your relationships with others. Be prepared to take a lowly position, as a humble servant; be prepared to pay the price of imitating the example of Jesus.

The passage is not really speaking to the question of whether Christians should be involved in legal or military professions. Rather, it is challenging believers to follow their Master's example in personal relationships. The illustrations Jesus uses seem to bear this out.

1. *Turn the other cheek*. Jesus pictures a man being slapped on the right cheek. Two things are significant about that. First, such a blow was more an insult than a violent crime. And insult it was, of massive proportions, for it was a blow with the back of the hand, something still regarded as grossly offensive in the Near East. The fine for such an insult exceeded the average man's annual wages. Second, it was an insult for which the only recourse was to take a man to court, as people might do today for libel or defamation of character.

What does Jesus mean when he says, 'Turn the other cheek'? Can Jesus be suggesting that the Christian deliberately put himself in the way of further suffering? No, Jesus is reminding his disciples in this figurative way that to stand on their 'rights' and seek to have their dignity reaffirmed is not the Christian response to any insult.

'Let the insults come,' says Jesus, 'and show by your response that you feel no need for retaliation, because you have your reputation secure with God, as his child. Let your response to insult be gracious – just as your Father's response to your insult of sin against him has been so gracious. Will anyone be won for the kingdom by your retaliation, by your standing on your rights?' How could they be, when the King in the kingdom is one who did not retaliate?

2. *Give away your tunic*. Here Jesus pictures a man sued for his tunic. Give your coat as well, Jesus adds. Almost certainly, he is simply expressing a basic principle as vividly as he can here. He does not mean a man should be left virtually naked! The point of the saying is clarified when we remember that the coat of the Jew was virtually sacrosanct. If it were taken as a financial pledge, it had to be returned before nightfall (*Ex. 22:24*), be-

cause for some it served as both body clothing and bed clothing.

Again, Jesus' point is that when his followers meet with opposition and persecution, they should not stand on their legal rights. Instead, where the sin of others abounds, grace in them should abound much more. In that, they will be like their Master (*see Rom. 5:20*).

3. *Go the extra mile.* The Roman army that occupied Palestine had the right to force people to assist them – for example, Simon of Cyrene was forced to carry Christ's cross (*Mk. 15:21*). The Jews hated the practice because it publicly illustrated the humiliation of being a subjugated people. We can easily imagine how open to abuse it was.

When you are 'drafted,' Jesus says, and have walked the one thousand paces required by the Roman regulations, keep going. Carry the load one more mile! No soldier has the right to make you do that. Do it voluntarily. Thus he may see that you have another Emperor, and belong to another Empire, with principles that are infinitely stronger than the laws of Rome!

Such Roman soldiers were not the last to feel the power of the principles of the kingdom of God illustrated so vividly. Recently I heard of the faithful witness of the daughter of a well-known Asian Christian. She had been imprisoned because of her Christian testimony. When influence to set her free was volunteered, she refused. She was reported to have said that she would rather remain in prison, where she was committed to bear witness to Jesus Christ. Far from seeking retaliation, she was prepared to sacrifice her right of freedom.

Jesus' point is clear: the Christian does the unexpected, because grace makes him or her seek to win others by love rather than retaliate on the basis of 'rights'.

4. *Give to those who beg or borrow.* Such giving was not a legal duty for these early disciples. They were under no

obligation to give. But Jesus is showing them that the law restraining evil acts is also meant to teach us to express a lifestyle of grace that is the opposite of the forbidden sin! This is the point Paul was to make later when he contrasted the works of the flesh with the fruit of the Spirit.

The works of the flesh disqualify us for the kingdom of God because they breach God's law (*Gal. 5:19–21*), but there is no law against the fruit of the Spirit, those graces whose opposites the law forbids! Love is the fulfilment of the law (*Rom. 13:10*). Only when we show gracious care and sacrifice for the sake of others will they see what the God-given meaning of the law really is. Then they will understand that our citizenship is in the kingdom of heaven (*Phil. 3:20*).

LOVE YOUR ENEMIES

God's word had taught that men were to love their neighbour (*Lev. 19:18*). It is interesting to notice that Scripture indicates no conflict between law and love here. Love is part of the law, and is commanded in the law! But, like so many biblical principles, this one had been first analysed and then distorted by the teachers of the law in the following way: not only is the law in itself true, but its opposite will be true. So, if we are to *love our neighbours*, it follows that we are to *hate our enemies*. Much discussion then took place to narrow down the answer to the question, Who is my neighbour?

When Jesus was asked that question (*Lk. 10:29*), he did not give an 'off the cuff' response. His reply was one of the great theological talking points of the day. Jesus' answer then, as his teaching here, was revolutionary in the moral challenge it presented to the disciples.

It is true that you are to love your neighbour, Jesus

affirms. But that law is intended to restrain your hatred, not to justify it against those you do not consider to be your neighbours. The law is only a starting place, the shadow cast on man's sinful life by God's original desire that we should love all men, and that in this fallen world we should even love our enemies.

Can we really love those who have been hostile to us? Not as long as we live by the principles of the kingdoms of this world, which at best encourage us to ignore our enemies, and at worst to retaliate against them. Only the kingdom of God can provide sufficiently strong motives to help us love our enemies: your Father shows love to his enemies every day in giving the sun and the rain to the righteous and the ungodly alike. He has every right to retaliate against sinners for the dishonour they have done to his creation. Instead, he shows mercy and patience. We are to do the same. Like Father, like son!

We can say in a special sense, 'Like Father, like Son.' This is not an empty, wishful thought for us, because the lifestyle Jesus encourages here is one he also exemplified. When his enemies sought to triumph over him, what did he do? He loved them, and prayed for them that they might be forgiven. His power to enable his people to do the same is illustrated in the life and death of Stephen (*Lk. 23:24; Acts 7:60*).

Jesus presses this point home with unusual force. If we love only those who love us, what is special about us? What shows that we are different? The tax collectors, that hated and ostracised segment of Jewish society, seen as traitors within the camp, do the same. Pagans follow that principle.

God's people should be different. It should be obvious that we are extra-ordinary, for our Father is extra-ordinary.

This is what Jesus means when he tell us to be 'perfect' like the Father. He is not assuming we can reach moral perfection in this life. Rather, he is reflecting on the way in which the love of the Father is demonstrated in its perfection in the way he loves his enemies. The man who does that shows that his love is not controlled by its object, but by his own will, and by his commitment to the Father's ways.

The mark of 'perfection' in the Christian is just this: his love is not determined by the loveliness or the attractiveness he finds in its object. His love is not conditional upon his being loved first. His love is not directed only towards those whose love he can rely on in return. No, his love is controlled by the knowledge that when he was God's enemy and a sinner, the Father first loved him. If he is to show the Father's love – the family love – then he will 'go and do likewise' (*Lk. 10:37*).

There is something haunting about the question Jesus asks in verse 47: 'What are you doing *more* than others?' He assumes that members of the kingdom and family of God will not behave 'like mere men' (*1 Cor. 3:4*). All that he has said in the description of the family of God in the Beatitudes confirms that we are not ordinary men. Different principles control our thinking and our living; we keep in step to the beat of a different drummer.

How tragic that the church has so often sought to be little different from the world, under the guise of attracting the world. But, there is more than that to such a compromise. It is rooted in an unwillingness to let Jesus Christ teach us the principles of his kingdom. For there is a high price to be paid for true Christian living. It costs *everything*.

In the final analysis, that is what Jesus means when he calls us to be perfect, like his Father. The teaching in Matthew 5:21–48 simply spells it out. The Father has given everything for us. He calls us to give everything for him and to him – no matter what it costs.

You see, there is only one basis on which a person can

love his neighbour as himself (which is the essence of Jesus' teaching in this section). You know what it is. Jesus has told you:

Love the Lord your God with all your heart and with all your soul and with all your strength and with all your mind.
(Lk. 10:27)

Do you? Honestly?

10
Life with Father

'Be careful not to do your "acts of righteousness" before men, to be seen by them. If you do, you will have no reward from your Father in heaven.

2'So when you give to the needy, do not announce it with trumpets, as the hypocrites do in the synagogues and on the streets, to be honoured by men. I tell you the truth, they have received their reward in full. 3But when you give to the needy, do not let your left hand know what your right hand is doing, 4so that your giving may be in secret. Then your Father, who sees what is done in secret, will reward you.

5'But when you pray, do not be like the hypocrites, for they love to pray standing in the synagogues and on the street corners to be seen by men. I tell you the truth, they have received their reward in full. 6When you pray, go into your room, close the door and pray to your Father, who is unseen. Then your Father, who sees what is done in secret, will reward you. 7And when you pray, do not keep on babbling like pagans, for they think they will be heard because of their many words. 8Do not be like them, for your Father knows what you need before you ask him.'

¹⁶'*When you fast, do not look sombre as the hypocrites do,
for they disfigure their faces to show men they are fasting. I tell
you the truth, they have received their reward in full.* ¹⁷*But
when you fast, put oil on your head and wash your face,* ¹⁸*so
that it will not be obvious to men that you are fasting, but only
to your Father, who is unseen; and your Father, who sees what
is done in secret, will reward you.*'

★　　★　　★

The transition from the fifth to the sixth chapters of
Matthew's Gospel introduces us to a new section of the
Sermon on the Mount. It also provides an appropriate
point for us to pause in our study of these chapters to
notice one of their most interesting features – what they
teach us about Jesus as a preacher and teacher.

Jesus is the model teacher and preacher in the church.
We should, therefore, notice both the content and the
style of his teaching if we are to learn to communicate the
gospel as he did.

This sermon has all of the marks of great teaching. In
the first place, it is marked by *unity* of theme. Jesus is
teaching us about life in the kingdom of God. Notice that
from the beginning of the sermon, when he describes
those who belong to the kingdom, to the end of the
sermon, when he challenges us about our own relationship
to the kingdom, he does not deviate from his theme. He
does not go off on a tangent. Rather, the weight and power
of his teaching – the 'authority' that its first audience
recognised (*Matt. 7:29*) – was the cumulative effect of its
unity. Jesus knew the human mind, and understood how
God had made men to think and understand. The fact that
Jesus' teaching was thus marked by unity of thought is
very significant for us.

But, in the second place, his teaching is characterised
by *progression* of thought. His sermon is not a series of

isolated elements, having one theme in common. In fact, it is not difficult to see how one unit in the sermon *builds* on what has gone before, expanding and developing the thrust of the message. The closing illustration of the wise builder and the foolish builder can be applied to Jesus himself as the master builder, or teacher. He digs down deeply to lay solid foundations in the Beatitudes and his teaching on the quality of the righteousness of God's people. Then he builds on that foundation a picture of the lifestyle of the Christian. All the time there is a development.

In the third place, Jesus used *wise illustrations* and *application*. Interestingly, his preaching was not illustrated by stories about himself (a characteristic of much preaching of only the last hundred years or so). Actually, Jesus' illustrations have a very different function from most present-day illustrations: they do not aim to entertain, although some of them are humorous, nor do they aim merely to keep people's attention. They are meant to open up the listener's conscience and help him to realise his true spiritual condition before God. That is why illustration and application go hand in hand in Jesus' sermon.

Those of us who teach or preach would do well to study these and other elements in our Lord's ministry, and to give time to examining how faithful our own approach to teaching is to that of our Master. Such an effort can be a very searching exercise, but it bears rich and lasting fruit in our Christian service.

Some of these features are particularly well illustrated in Matthew 6:1–18. Jesus had emphasised the *quality* of the righteousness of his disciples (*5:20*). He illustrated this in terms of the teaching of God's law. In Matthew 5:21–48 he expounded its profound spiritual and moral significance. The righteousness God seeks is in the heart.

[108]

It is not peripheral and superficial, but thorough and lasting.

How tempting for some of his hearers to think: 'This is wonderful – a righteousness that is inward. We can forget about discipline. That is what these Pharisees think is so necessary to true spiritual well-being. Let us instead be inwardly pure and holy.'

But Jesus does not draw a dichotomy between 'outward' and 'inward.' The truly righteous man shows his righteousness in righteous deeds. Furthermore, true righteousness is expressed, says Jesus, in the disciplines of the believer. Jesus calls these 'acts of righteousness' (*6:1*). He does not say, 'Be careful not to do your "acts of righteousness."' He does not even say, 'Be careful not to do your "acts of righteousness" before men.' He actually says, 'Be careful not to do your "acts of righteousness" before men, *to be seen by them.*'

In saying this, Jesus is directing attention to motives. *Why* we do something is significant as well as *what* we do.

Jesus also clears away another general misconception by what he says here. The principle he expounds in Matthew 6:1 is illustrated in three different ways: *giving (6:2–4)*, *praying (6:5–15)*, and *fasting (6:16–18)*. He indicates in what he says about each of these activities that sacrifice, self-discipline, and self-denial are called for in the Christian life. He assumes that our lives will be well regulated, properly structured, and that we will show an increasing mastery of our own desires. *Jesus does not assume that these things will come 'naturally'.* Rather, he sees them as quite deliberate activities in the life of his disciples.

To an unusual degree today, Christians mistakenly think that the freedom of Christian experience means that we no longer need to make any effort to be spiritual. We simply 'do what we feel,' and 'be ourselves'. To live any other way – for example, to set aside definite and sacrificial amounts of money to the Lord's work, or to set aside specific time during the day for prayer, or to enage in deliberate acts of self-denial as we seek the Lord's face – is seen as 'legalism' and 'bondage.' Jesus, on the other hand, assumes that these disciplines are basic to any spiritual vitality. And he was no legalist!

Beyond these general lessons that we can learn, we must also focus attention on the specifics of Jesus' teaching here. It can be divided into three elements: the illustrations he uses; the spiritual danger he describes; and the remedy he prescribes.

ILLUSTRATIONS

Jesus gives us three vivid illustrations: our relationship to others in our giving; our relationship to our needs in our praying; and our relationship to ourselves in private fasting. Each illustration indicates that our fundamental relationship is to God.

Jesus describes a man who is the essence of charity – or so he would like others to think. He plans to give a gift. So he hires a musician – a trumpeter. After all, if he is going to give to the poor, he will need to call their attention to his provision. Why else would a man hire a trumpeter and give his gift publicly? Why else, indeed!

But, says Jesus, this is not a gift in the sight of God. It is *a purchase*! The man is not *helping* the poor half as much as he is *using* the poor to help him. He has received his reward in full (*6:2*). The language Matthew uses here is the same language that appeared on settled accounts in the ancient world. When such men are seen by their fellows, then God writes over their lives, 'Paid in full.'

We do not need trumpets any longer. We call press conferences instead. Why is it that donors (large and small) seem to feel a need for people to know of their donations? Of course, *the amount* remains undisclosed. After all, one shouldn't give to the needy in public! People might think we did it for the sake of our reputation.

Even those of us who are in no position to call press conferences or hand out press releases can still find ways of 'letting it slip' that we give to 'the cause.' Sometimes the most subtle way to do so is by letting others know how much blessing we have received since we started to give a certain percent of our income (our *gross* income, of course!). How subtle our desire for reputation is.

Give! Jesus says. But when you do so, *forget about yourself*. And *forget about others*. Keep it between yourself and the Lord, and do it 'as unto the Lord.'

Jesus talks about another man. He is not ashamed that he is a man of prayer. In fact, he is never more excited than when he can pray in the prayer meeting. He is obviously a 'man of prayer'.

Unfortunately, he prays more in public than he does in private. Also, he prays more eloquently, more fervently, more intimately, in public than he does in private. Can it possibly be that all of his zeal for prayer is motivated by his desire 'to be seen by men' (*Matt. 6:5*)? He certainly receives what he wants.

Pray! Jesus says. But when you do, *forget about yourself*. And *forget about others*. Lock yourself in, secretly, quietly, with the Lord. He sees what you do in secret, and that is all that really matters.

Jesus talks about yet another man. He is known for his enormous self-discipline. But wait a minute! Does he always look so sombre because of his great efforts at self-discipline? Does that expression on his face need to be so depressing as he sees children laugh and play? Yet there is no denying how godly he must be. Nobody has ever seen him smile.

There is more than one way for hypocrites to 'disfigure their faces' (*6:16*). The man who so desires can let it be known how demanding he finds it to serve the Lord. He will have his reward. There are still plenty of gullible people who will be taken in.

Fast! Jesus says. Such self-discipline is essential in the Christian life. But when you do, be a normal human being. Take a shower. Use some aftershave, and smile (*6:17!*). Do your fasting before the Lord, not before men.

THE DANGER

These are vivid illustrations. Jesus wants to point out to his disciples that there are dangers in the spiritual life when sinners undertake it. Conversion does not remove the presence of sin from our hearts, even though it is dethroned in our lives. Sin still works deceitfully in our minds.

Jesus certainly had the Pharisees in mind when he used these word pictures. The Pharisees were 'lay' people who had formed a movement two hundred years before Christ's ministry. They were always a minority, but they apparently gathered together in convention form to strengthen one another in their great mission. They were concerned about purity. Practical holiness was their goal. In particular, their lives were marked by good works of charity, regular prayer (three hours each day), and tithing. They were, essentially, a 'holiness movement,' as the name, Pharisee ('separated one') suggests.

Jesus' view of the Pharisees should act as a warning beacon to evangelical Christians. There may be a special temptation to which those who are zealous for holy living can fall prey: retaining the outward shell of spiritual life; emphasising the importance of certain supposed 'marks of grace,' but lacking the power and grace of God. Many

Christians begin well in their quest for holy lives, as the Pharisees did, but become ensnared by their desire to have a reputation before men rather than before God.

These men had become 'hypocrites' (*6:2, 5, 16*). The Greek word Matthew uses here – *hupokritēs* – illuminates what Jesus is talking about. It is a word from the world of the theatre, and suggests the nature of the problem with these men. Their religion was theatrical, rather than genuine.

In ancient drama, an important part of a play was fulfilled by the chorus. As in opera and musicals, it provided commentary on the action of the play. In fact, the *hupokritēs* was, 'the one who answered the chorus.' That is exactly what the Pharisees had begun to do. Their religious activities were no longer answering to God. Instead their eyes were fixed on the 'chorus' of men's opinion of them.

In ancient drama, actors did not wear make-up. They wore masks, representing the parts they played. What a vivid picture that gives us of the hypocrite. He pretends to be one thing, but all the time he is really something altogether different. His outward actions suggest that his whole heart is focused on the Lord, but his inward desires are for the recognition and the praise of men.

It is so easy to hide this hypocrisy, yet so difficult to deal with it. It is deep-rooted in the human heart. We recognise it in our own response to praise or criticism. We might modestly say all the right 'spiritual' things when people praise our service, but inwardly drink it in like thirsty men. We might receive criticism with apparent humility, yet inwardly seethe with resentment and determine never to forget the hurt we have received. In either case, we forget that the only thing that matters is what God thinks.

THE REMEDY

Why do men become like this? Why do *we* become like this? There may be several answers to that question.

We fail to understand and deal with our own hearts. This is one of the most frequent mistakes Christians make. We fall prey to what the New Testament calls 'sin's deceitfulness' (*Heb. 3:13*).

How does sin deceive us? We fail to take seriously its continuing presence in our hearts, and consequently treat lightly the biblical teaching that sin needs to be mortified in our hearts through the power of the Spirit (*Rom. 8:13*).

We need to keep a strict hold on our hearts, lest we drift into Pharisaism. We begin to get a taste for 'having a reputation,' and we no longer see what we are in secret before God (*Matt. 6:6*) as so very vital.

In the context of the Sermon on the Mount, Jesus directs us to an altogether different reason for the spiritual hypocrisy he sees in the Pharisees. Notice that in Matthew 6:1–18, God is called 'Father' on ten different occasions. Throughout this section of the sermon, our Lord hints that the real trouble with the heart of the hypocrite is that he does not know God as his heavenly Father! He is *insecure* before God and, therefore, seeks security in what his fellow men think about him. He is unreal in his activities before men because he has no real relationship with God.

The more you read the Gospel narratives, the more you will become convinced that this was a chief reason for Jesus' controversy with the Pharisees. He was not against disciplines in the Christian life. The reason he reserved his strongest condemnations for Pharisees (*Matt. 23*) was because they distorted the character of his Father, and turned him into a tyrant, a slave driver who did nothing but place restrictive burdens on his people. By distorting the image of God, they 'shut the kingdom of heaven in men's faces' (*Matt. 23:13*). They did not know God as Father at all, and they hated the thought that he should show mercy to sinners who had broken his law.

The parable we know as 'The Prodigal Son' deals with this theme. It is set in this context: 'The Pharisees and the teachers of the law muttered, "This man welcomes sinners and eats with them"' (*Lk. 15:2*). The attitude of the Pharisees to sinners is contrasted with the attitude of the father. Whereas the father welcomed home the prodigal with open arms and expressions of forgiveness and love, the elder brother 'became angry and refused to go in' to the party the father was giving (*Lk. 15:28*). Despite the father's pleas, the brother retorted, 'Look! All these years *I've been slaving for you* and never disobeyed your orders' (*Lk. 15:29*).

Likewise, the Pharisees thought God was a slave driver, not a Father. They had never entered into a gracious relationship with him themselves. They wanted to make sure that nobody else would, either.

Jesus spoke powerfully against them: 'Woe to you, teachers of the law and Pharisees, you hypocrites! You travel over land and sea to win a single convert, and when he becomes one, you make him twice as much a son of hell as you are' (*Matt. 23:15*). They were distorting the truth about God the Father, and as a direct result, keeping men from knowing his grace and pardon. They were graceless, and therefore damned, and they dragged others to hell with them. No wonder our Lord was angry.

This sense of insecurity before God, this view of him as a slave driver and tyrant goes back in history long before the Pharisees. They had taken sides with Satan by subscribing to the view that he had expounded in the Garden of Eden: 'God has set you in this magnificent garden, but he means to use you as slaves, to restrict your lives and your liberty, because he has forbidden you to eat from *any* of the trees in the Garden' (*see Gen. 3:1*).

But that was a *lie*. God had given Adam and Eve liberty to enjoy the whole garden, but forbidden them to take from the tree of the knowledge of good and evil (*see Gen. 2:16–17*). The Lord had been a Father to man in his lavish provision and blessing. But Satan insinuated God was a miser.

The Pharisees thought of God in the same way. They 'slaved' for him in the mistaken assumption that they might thus gain a standing with him. The tragedy was that they did not really know who God was at all. They *dis-graced* the Father. That is why, in the parable of the prodigal son, the brother is depicted as hating the father, hating the father's grace, and hating his once-lost brother.

The Pharisees' view of God is shared by all men by nature. Even Jesus' disciples can find it lingering in their own hearts. And when it is, Satan will do all in his power to accentuate it. That is why, over and over again in this section, Jesus refers to God as 'your Father.' We will never escape from spiritual bondage until we are thoroughly convinced of that. Only when we know God as 'Father' can we be secure in his presence and fellowship.

The hypocrite looks for a reward. He finds security in the knowledge that men think highly of him. But that is all the reward he will ever receive, says Jesus.

By contrast, the disciple does not lose his reward. His desire is to be thought well of by his Father. When the disciple gives because he loves his Father, or prays because he trusts his Father's care about his needs, or fasts because he longs to submit his whole being to his Father's will, he has his reward: 'Your Father, who sees what is done in secret, will reward you' (*Matt. 6:4, 6, 18*).

What kind of reward are you looking for? Your answer will depend on how you think of God – as your slave master, or as your Father.

11
How to Pray and Live

⁹"This is how you should pray:
"Our Father in heaven,
hallowed be your name,
¹⁰your kingdom come,
your will be done
    on earth as it is in heaven.
¹¹Give us today our daily bread.
¹²Forgive us our debts,
    as we also have forgiven our debtors.
¹³And lead us not into temptation,
    but deliver us from the evil one."
¹⁴For if you forgive men when they sin against you, your
heavenly Father will also forgive you. ¹⁵But if you do not
forgive men their sins, your Father will not forgive your sins.'

★　　★　　★

Jesus has already made it clear in Matthew 6 that the single most important influence on the way we live the Christian life is *how we think of God*. For Jesus, *theology* (how we think about God) determines *practice* (how we live our lives). In particular, Jesus stressed how important it is for us to think of God as Father, and to know the intimacy of a Father-son relationship with him. J.I. Packer has summarised it in these words:

> *You sum up the whole of the New Testament teaching in a single phrase, if you speak of it as a revelation of the Fatherhood of the holy Creator. In the same way you sum up the whole of New Testament religion if you describe it as the knowledge of God as one's holy Father. If you want to judge how well a person understands Christianity, find out how much he makes of the thought of being God's child, and having God as his Father. If this is not the thought that prompts and controls his worship and prayers and his whole outlook on life, it means that he does not understand Christianity very well at all.*[1]

That is precisely what Jesus is saying in Matthew 6 when he exposes the religion of the hypocrites and pagans for what it really is: ignorance of God. The way they speak in prayer underlines the fact that they do not know God as Father. The contrast between them and those of us who belong to the kingdom of God is that we are to know the Great King as Father in heaven.

All this, in a sense, is familiar to Christians. Yet, as this whole section of Jesus' sermon shows us, perhaps we more often *assume* it than *experience* it. Otherwise our Christian lives would have a more gracious, more joyful, more stable, more caring quality altogether. And, in particular, we would know better what it means *to pray*. Rather than hide from God in our hypocrisy (like the Pharisees) or mistrust him in our anxiety (like the pagans), we would

[1] J.I. Packer, *Knowing God*, Hodder and Stoughton, London, 1973, p. 182.

cast all our cares on him, because we know he cares for us (*1 Pet. 5:7*).

There is, of course, a paradox here. Even as Christians, we have an instinct to hide from the Father, both because he is the Great King and because we are still sinners. Any human father knows that his children are sometimes ashamed of what they have done, realise they deserve to be chastised, and hide their secrets in fear. Furthermore, life is uncertain and full of trials. We are often anxious. Until we are brought into the kingdom of glory, experiences which can evoke anxiety will be part and parcel of our lives. So long as this is true, coming to the Father will involve us in a strange conflict: the pain and shame of our failure will mix with the joy and relief of his great grace.

That is why the ancient church prayed the Lord's Prayer with these words of introduction: 'Grant that we may *dare* to call on thee as Father, and to say, "Our Father"' (Liturgy of St. Chrysostom). They recognised the paradox that fellowship with God in his prayer means sorrow for our sin, yet joy in his forgiveness and grace. Prayer involves struggle, but the struggle is not that of persuading our God. Rather, it is the struggle involved in being subdued by God, coming out of the dark and secret places in which we have been hiding the truth about ourselves, and laying the whole of our lives before him.

Jesus knew this, and, therefore, taught his disciples to pray by means of what we call 'The Lord's Prayer.' It serves two purposes. First, it provides a model prayer, an easily memorised outline, that serves as a lesson in how we are to approach God as Father and how we are to speak with him. Second, it serves as an outline of the whole Christian life by providing certain 'fixed points' of concern for the family of God. It underlines life's priorities and helps us to get them into focus.

(Sometimes Christians are critical of the title 'The Lord's Prayer' on the grounds that Jesus himself did not use it. He would not have asked for his debts to be forgiven, since he was without sin. But this is to miss the meaning of the title. It does not suggest that Jesus *prayed* these words, but that he *taught* them.)

The prayer focuses on five concepts: the *worship* of the Father; the *kingdom* of the Father; the *sustenance* of the Father; the *grace* of the Father; and the *protection* of the Father.

THE WORSHIP OF THE FATHER

In the opening petitions of his prayer, Jesus brings together two ideas that are true *only* of royal children: the intimacy of children, and access to the Great King. The one we address in prayer is *in heaven*, and yet he is 'our Father.' The whole of our worship flows from these few words. They, in turn, invest our worship with the grandeur and the joy of true praise and adoration.

Jesus is clearly stressing the greatness of God in his heavenly glory, and what we sometimes call the Creator-creature distinction: he is in heaven, while we are on the earth; he is heavenly, while we are earthly; he is the eternal one, while we are his creatures, made by him and dependent upon him for every breath we breathe. This is why we pray, 'Hallowed be your name.' It is not that God's name can in itself be made more holy than it is. But rather, we are reminded how much we need his help to recognise just how holy, or separate from us, he really is. And, indeed, we even need his help to come to him with the sense of awe and wonder that is appropriate for his glory.

At the same time, we *dare* to call on him as Father! We know that he is near us and cares for us in a special way because he has given us life as our Creator, and new life as our Saviour. Every believer confesses to the Lord, 'You created my inmost being; you knit me together in my mother's womb' (*Ps. 139:13*). But we must also confess that when we were spiritually dead, the Lord brought us into new life (*Eph. 2:1–5*) by giving us a new birth (*1 Pet. 1:23*). We are his privileged children.

Furthermore, these words underline the fellowship and corporate nature of the Christian life. We pray, 'Our Father,' not 'My Father' – not only because Jesus prayed, 'My Father,' and we should distinguish ourselves from him, but to remind us that we share our spiritual privileges with all the people of God. That in itself adds to the privileges that we receive.

Notice the balance of this teaching. It contains three elements: *intimacy* (*'Father'*), *adoration* (*'in Heaven'*), *and fellowship* ('our'), and thereby sets the tone for Christian living, and especially for our praying. We do not live in intimacy with God in a way that destroys our reverence for him or in a manner that isolates us from our fellow Christians. If we were to write these few words over the whole of our lives, their truth and power would transform our relationship to God, to ourselves, and to others.

These words also concentrate our attention on the glory of God in the sanctifying of his name. This includes our speech. We do not trample the Lord's name in the dust by using it loosely. By doing so, we would show that we do not really know him. Who would use the name of someone he admired and loved as a curse? It is unthinkable.

But the real issue goes far beyond speech, to that of which our speech is the expression. We are praying here that God will be glorified in all things. We are recognising, as the *Shorter Catechism* says, that 'man's chief end is to glorify God and to enjoy him for ever.' We are really saying about our own lives, 'Lord, may everything I do and say show forth your glory as my Father in heaven, and may all my thoughts be focused on what will bring honour to your name.'

If this is true, can you even begin to pray this prayer? When Martin Luther was climbing the Sancta Scala (the supposed staircase Christ climbed to his judgment before Pilate), and saying the Lord's Prayer on his knees, he is reputed to have managed to pray no farther than 'Thy will.' But can we pray even so far as those words? Only if our lives are given over to the glory of God!

THE KINGDOM OF THE FATHER

The secret of the kingdom of God is that it is ruled by the Father. Out of our love for him and our concern for his glory, we pray that his kingdom will come.

We have already seen that there is a present reality about the kingdom of God. It has come in Jesus. But there is also a sense in which it has not yet come in its full glory. Its final flowering is still awaited. We live now between the inauguration of the kingdom and the consummation of the kingdom. We therefore pray that the kingdom that has already been established will express its presence more and more throughout the earth, until the day comes when 'the kingdom of the world has become the kingdom of our Lord and of his Christ, and he will reign for ever and ever' (*Rev. 11:15*).

New Testament Christians were often far more conscious of what this meant than we are today. In fact, a great deal of Paul's teaching (as well as that of Jesus) is dominated by this thought: we are to live as those who have already experienced the power of Christ's kingly rule, yet who still long for its completion. Because we live 'in between the times,' we fight, and labour, and sometimes struggle.

We are those who have received the Spirit of Christ and

his kingdom (*Rom. 8:9*), but that is the very reason we have to struggle to deal death blows to the sin that remains in our lives (*Rom. 8:13*). We have already received the Spirit of sons (*Rom. 8:15*), and know that we are heirs together with Christ (*Rom. 8:17*), but because we belong to his family, we must share in his sufferings. That is why – precisely because we have the Spirit of Christ – we 'groan' as we wait for the day when the kingdom of God will be established fully and finally (*Rom. 8:23*).

This, then, is what lies behind Jesus telling us that we are to pray, with urgency, 'Your kingdom come, your will be done on earth as it is in heaven.' Think what this involves.

1. *Bowing to God's sovereign purposes.* Jesus not only taught his disciples to pray, 'Your will be done,' he established the kingdom by praying these words himself in the garden of Gethsemane, when he accepted 'the cup' that his Father was giving him to drink (*Matt. 26:39*). For Jesus, seeking first the kingdom of God, praying for it to come, meant taking up the cross, dying for others, and thus yielding his life in complete obedience to God.

In this way, Jesus exposes the heart of the petition he taught his disciples to pray. For God establishes his kingdom through the cross, first of all by Jesus dying on it, and then by Jesus' disciples taking it up daily as his followers. Unlike the kings of this world, God establishes his kingdom through suffering, self-denial, and service! To pray for that kingdom means committing yourself to the way of the cross.

2. *Seeking the spread of the gospel.* The kingdom of God comes inwardly, but the children of God also ask for it to spread outwardly – geographically. The Lord's Prayer is a *missionary* prayer. As a model prayer, it teaches us to put the spread of the gospel before our own needs (and perhaps even the support of world missions which *includes*

local evangelism – further up the scale of priorities than we tend to do).

In one sense, this is already implicit in the corporate address Jesus teaches us to use: 'Our Father.' We cannot address him in this way without recognising that we belong to a family that encircles the globe and stretches back into the past and forward into the future. It is interesting that in his last prayer with his disciples before his passion, Jesus himself prayed in these terms: 'My prayer is not for them alone. I pray also for those who will believe in me through their message' (*Jn. 17:20*).

Jesus, who was himself a missionary sent by the Father into the world, prays for other missionaries and *for those who believe through them*. How often our missionary prayers are only for our missionaries and workers! If we really followed Jesus' example in praying this petition, would we not also want to know more intimately and pray more definitely for those who are brought into our family through our brothers and sisters?

3. *Searching out God's will in Scripture*. When we pray that God's will should be done, we are not blindly committing ourselves to 'let things happen' with a fatalistic *que sera sera* attitude! No, such a prayer implies that we ourselves will seek out and then do the will of God. In a nutshell, we discover that will as we become familiar with God's revealed will in Scripture and subsequently develop the wisdom to apply biblical teaching to the different situations and experiences of our lives.

Again, we should notice that Jesus is our model in this regard. The Gospels indicate that he saw the will of God for his own life by applying the teaching of the Old Testament. When he was tempted by Satan in the wilderness, he relied on God's will revealed in Scripture (and rightly applied – unlike Satan's use of Scripture).

Throughout his ministry he applied to himself Isaiah's

prophetic description of the Servant of the Lord (*Is. 42:1–8; 49:1–7; 50:4–11; 52:13–53:12*) and the prophecies of his death (*e.g. 26:24,31,54,56*). Few things are more obvious about his life than the fact that he was steeped in Scripture. When he prayed, 'Your will be done' in the garden of Gethsemane, he knew – from Scripture – what that would mean.

Have you followed that example? It is a key element in knowing the will of God in order to be obedient to it. It is the secret of the Lord's guidance, as John Newton well knew:

> *How then may the Lord's guidance be expected? . . . In general, he guides and directs his people, by affording them, in answer to prayer, the light of his Holy Spirit, which enables them to understand and to love the Scriptures. The word of God is not to be used as a lottery; nor is it designed to instruct us by shreds and scraps, which, detached from their proper places, have no determinate import; but it is to furnish us with just principles, right apprehensions to regulate our judgments and affections, and thereby influence and direct our conduct.* [2]

It is in this way that we are able, intelligently to pray, 'Your will be done.'

4. *Praying for Christ's return.* The coming of the kingdom and the return of the King belong together. When we pray, 'Your kingdom come,' we are asking the Father to do what we know he most certainly will do – bring to a final denouement the history of the human race and usher in the new age of his glory.

Only the children of God can have this view of the future. Only Christians can be long-term optimists, and live without debilitating anxiety because they know that their own lives and the history of the world have a final

[2]*The Letters of John Newton*, pp. 81–2.

destiny that Jesus Christ controls (see *Revelation 5*). That prospect influences the way we live here and now. No one can rightly pray, 'Your kingdom come' or 'Come, Lord Jesus' (*Rev. 22:20*) without *here and now* bringing his life into conformity with the will of God.

In fact, that is the single most frequent application of the promise of the Lord's return in the teaching of the New Testament (see for example: *Mk. 13:32–37; 1 Cor. 15:58; 1 Thess. 5:1–11; 2 Pet. 3:8–14*). Again and again we discover that all the facets involved in praying, 'Your will be done' imply that our lives are submitted to the Lord Jesus Christ here and now.

THE SUSTENANCE OF THE FATHER

Christians have long realised that there is a clear order to the Lord's Prayer. Its opening focus is God and his glory. Only then does it move to man and his need.

There is an obvious reason for this: God and his kingdom must always take priority over man and his needs. That certainly needs to be underscored, but it should never be stated in isolation from another biblical truth. Since man was made for the glory of God, he can never be what he is intended to be until his life is properly focused on the glory of God. Unless our vision of life *is* properly focused, the whole of life will be more or less distorted. Jesus makes this point very vividly later in his sermon (*Matt. 6:22–23*).

So God's glory does not detract from man's life. Instead, his glory is the sun around which the whole of life must revolve if there is to be the light and life of God in our experience. Since we were made for his glory, we will always malfunction whenever we fail to live for that purpose and according to the Maker's instructions.

In the light of this, we are encouraged to pray for our

'daily bread.' Far from being trivial, this prayer is intimately related to God's glory. Our eating and drinking – everything we do – are to be 'for the glory of God' (*1 Cor. 10:31*).

In the Western World we have become so accustomed to our extraordinary affluence that for many of us this petition has lost its power. That can only be because we have lost a biblical view of life. The food we eat is ours only because God upholds our universe and gives us seedtime and harvest. But beyond that, the food we eat *nourishes* us only because of his blessing. Today, more than ever before, we recognise that 'we are what we eat'! Even the most affluent of us, therefore, needs to pray that in his providence, God will make our food (and *our meals together*) occasions of blessing and strength.

Undoubtedly this petition includes our prayer for God's blessing on our food. But it means more, although the meaning is somewhat hidden by the usual translation 'our *daily* bread.'

Many scholars believe that the word translated 'daily' means not 'today's,' but 'tomorrow's.' The translation 'daily' is not inaccurate, then, but perhaps a little vague and undefined. In this case, what we are praying for is 'bread for tomorrow,' not only in the material sense of food and drink, but in the profound sense of food for God's 'tomorrow.' We are really asking for the blessings of the last days to be given to us now!

Elsewhere in the New Testament we discover that this prayer was answered for the church. It is the community on which the 'fulfilment of the ages has come' (*1 Cor. 10:11*), and which has 'tasted the goodness of the word of God and the powers of the coming age' (*Heb. 6:5*). Although the kingdom of God has not finally come, we are already encouraged to ask for its power in our lives through the Holy Spirit.

Although it is unlikely that Jesus is here referring to the bread of the Lord's supper, that occasion does provide us with the most vivid illustration of what he means in his prayer. In the Lord's supper we receive the bread and wine – ordinary food – but in doing so, our hearts are lifted beyond these signs to the one they represent, and we have communion with Christ. That is just a foretaste of our future fellowship with him. It is 'tomorrow's bread' tasted today, as it were. This is our Lord's promise to his people for the here-and-now: 'Here I am! I stand at the door and knock. If anyone hears my voice and opens the door, I will come in and eat with him, and he with me' (*Rev. 3:20*).

If we have all the food in the world, but no Christ, we will ultimately starve. If we have food, with Christ, we have all we shall ever need. Because we need *both*, we daily pray, 'Give us today our daily bread.'

THE GRACE OF THE FATHER

We are sometimes urged to pray on the grounds that prayer is 'easy.' But there is no hint of that in Scripture. True, we do not have to *merit* entrance into the presence of God. True, we come to a God who is our Father. But it is also true that we come as those who are conscious that we have brought clouds of sin into our relationship with him, and often all but obliterated the rays of his grace. To suggest that prayer should always be easy for sinners is, therefore, naïve and less than a biblical way to think.

Jesus is more realistic. That is why he teaches his disciples to pray, 'Forgive us our debts.' He knows that we come to our Father with the burden and nagging pain of our guilt. Jesus teaches us to keep what earlier Christians called 'short accounts' with God. We ask for forgiveness. We specify whatever debts we know we have.

We no longer foolishly try to hide them from the Lord. We admit them, bring them to the surface, mention them by name in his presence, and ask to be forgiven.

But Jesus adds a qualification to this petition: 'Forgive us our debts, *as we also have forgiven our debtors.*' So important is it that he enlarges on it: 'For if you forgive men when they sin against you, your heavenly Father will also forgive you. But if you do not forgive men their sins, your Father will not forgive your sins' (6:14–15).

Does Jesus mean that our *reception* of forgiveness is determined by our *granting* of forgiveness? That might seem to contradict the rest of the New Testament. Yet, Jesus does stress that without our forgiveness of others, there can be no forgiveness from God.

The key to understanding his teaching is to recognise that we do not receive forgiveness *because* we forgive others, but because we cast ourselves on the mercy of God. Yet we cannot receive forgiveness without forgiving others. The man who mouths the words 'Forgive us our debts,' but will not forgive others their debts, has not begun to understand the weight of his own sin. If he did, in the light of it being forgiven, he would be prepared to forgive his brother 'seventy-seven times' (*Matt. 18:22*).

If the words 'as we also have forgiven our debtors' stick in our throats; if they cannot be spoken without the names and faces of those we have refused to forgive coming into our minds, then the first part of our prayer, 'Forgive us our debts,' falls to the ground. The two are inseparably linked, for the man who knows his debt before God and turns to him for forgiveness is the recipient of such grace that he cannot but share it with others. Since God so loved us, we also ought to love one another with the love of forgiveness (*1 Jn. 4:11*).

THE PROTECTION OF THE FATHER

The final petition of the Lord's Prayer assumes that the children of God realise their weakness and vulnerability, and, therefore, seek the protection of God from evil. But the details of the final petition require closer study. Does the request not to be led into temptation assume that God may so lead us? What does it mean to be led *into* temptation? And what is involved in being delivered from evil, or from the Evil One?

The key to this petition is to be found in our Lord's personal experience. In the previous chapter of the Gospel, Matthew recorded the temptation of Jesus himself (*4:1–11*). It is a passage with several unique features, one of them being that the narrative must have come from the lips of Jesus himself. Apparently no one was with him during this long period of fasting and temptation. The intensity of the conflict he experienced must have been shared with the disciples after the event. Since that is so, the summary statement with which Matthew's account begins (*cf. Lk. 4:1–2*) should be understood as Jesus' own interpretation of what happened: He was '*led by the Spirit* into the desert *to be tempted by the devil.*' The devil tempted him. But even in that context, Jesus was led by God's Spirit.

It is difficult to avoid the conclusion that Jesus is teaching us here to pray that we will be protected from such an experience. Furthermore, that test was but the forerunner of the greater test to which the devil put Jesus later when he returned at a more opportune time (*Lk. 4:13*), when Jesus himself said that 'darkness reigns' (*Lk. 22:53*). Just as his baptism in the Jordan River foreshadowed his baptism in blood on the cross, so his testing in the wilderness was the forerunner of the terrible test he would face in Gethsemane and on Calvary.

We are to pray that we will be delivered from the Evil One now, and kept from the test of his full onslaught against our lives; that we will either be protected from such terrible testing, or, should we be faced with it in the providence of God, that we will be protected in it with the armour of God (*Eph. 6:10–20*).

Scripture describes both of these elements of testing with great vividness. It reminds us that we are exposed to the influence of the world, the flesh, and the devil. We can deal with the flesh by God's grace, or with the world and its allurements, and even with the devil in the strength of Christ. But the ultimate test confronts us when all three conspire together.

Who is able to stand when indwelling sin is incited by the temptations of the world and worldly people, and stirred up by the activity of Satan, either spurring us on to sin or hiding its dire consequences from us? This is the 'evil day' of which Paul spoke, for which we need the 'full armour of God' if we are to remain standing. That evil day is itself a shadow of the last great battle of the kingdom of God, the ultimate, eschatological evil day, from which we pray to be spared.

Jesus urges us to pray to be delivered. The fact that he does so assures us that our Father is both willing and able to deliver us. We know, with Paul, that 'the Lord will rescue me from every evil attack and will bring me safely to his heavenly kingdom. To him be glory for ever and ever' (*2 Tim. 4:18*).

We are weak, but he is strong. The Christian who does not know his weakness can, therefore, neither pray this prayer nor experience God's strength. The Christian who knows his weakness, but is a *praying* Christian, will be garrisoned by the Lord's strength. No wonder the ancient church added its own doxology to the Lord's Prayer:

For yours is the kingdom
and the power
and the glory
forever.
Amen.

12
Anxiety States
Cured

MATTHEW 6

[19]*Do not store up for yourselves treasures on earth, where moth and rust destroy, and where thieves break in and steal.* [20]*But store up for yourselves treasures in heaven, where moth and rust do not destroy, and where thieves do not break in and steal.* [21]*For where your treasure is, there your heart will be also.*

[22]*The eye is the lamp of the body. If your eyes are good, your whole body will be full of light.* [23]*But if your eyes are bad, your whole body will be full of darkness. If then the light within you is darkness, how great is that darkness!*

[24]*No one can serve two masters. Either he will hate the one and love the other, or he will be devoted to the one and despise the other. You cannot serve both God and Money.*

[25]*Therefore I tell you, do not worry about your life, what you will eat or drink; or about your body, what you will wear. Is not life more important than food, and the body more important than clothes?* [26]*Look at the birds of the air; they do not sow or reap or store away in barns, and yet your heavenly Father feeds them. Are you not much more valuable than they?* [27]*Who of you by worrying can add a single hour to his life?*

²⁸'*And why do you worry about clothes? See how the lilies of the field grow. They do not labour or spin.* ²⁹*Yet I tell you that not even Solomon in all his splendour was dressed like one of these.* ³⁰*If that is how God clothes the grass of the field, which is here today and tomorrow is thrown into the fire, will he not much more clothe you, O you of little faith?* ³¹*So do not worry, saying, "What shall we eat?" or "What shall we drink?" or "What shall we wear?"* ³²*For the pagans run after all these things, and your heavenly Father knows that you need them.* ³³*But seek first his kingdom and his righteousness, and all these things will be given to you as well.* ³⁴*Therefore do not worry about tomorrow, for tomorrow will worry about itself. Each day has enough trouble of its own.*'

*   *   *

At first glance, it seems strange that Jesus should develop his sermon by speaking first of *hypocrisy* and then of *anxiety* in Matthew chapter 6. But, that is exactly what he does. If the theme of verses 1–18 is, 'Do not be like the hypocrites,' the theme of the following section is, 'Do not be anxious. There is no need to worry' (*6:25,28,31*).

Yet a minute's reflection tells us that there is sound insight in Jesus' teaching at this point. Hypocrisy and anxiety are not so far apart as we might think. The *cause* of both is similar. So is the *cure*.

Why do people become anxious? In part, for the same reason they become hypocritical: they focus on self rather than on God. In the case of the hypocrite, the concern is to be seen by others. In the case of the anxious person, the concern is to supply his own needs. The hypocritical person and the anxious person probably have something else in common. Neither has really grasped the fact of the grace of God.

The cure for hypocrisy is, we have ready seen, the recognition that our Father knows, sees, and understands our lives. He cares for us, and accepts us as we are in Christ. He plans to change us. But that transformation grows out of his acceptance (grace); that transformation does not produce his acceptance (merit). The cure for anxiety is the same, as Jesus makes very clear in this section of the sermon. Particularly in verses 25–32, he reiterates the confidence we can have in our Father and in his perfect provision for all of our needs.

Jesus' teaching, then, is not a form of 'the power of positive thinking.' The problem with anxious people is not merely that they think *negatively* about life. It is much more radical than that. Anxious people think *untheologically* about life! Their mistake is not that they have low self-images; it is that 'in all their thoughts there is no room for God' (*Ps. 10:4*). It is only when their focus upon the Lord is restored that they can finally experience the conquest of anxiety.

We can develop this in detail, as Jesus himself did, by looking at his diagnosis of the causes of anxiety, and then at his prescription for its cure.

JESUS' DIAGNOSIS

Jesus knows men's hearts (*Jn. 2:24–25*). He is the Word of God that 'judges the thoughts and attitudes of the heart' (*Heb. 4:12*). We see that here. With clinical precision, he outlines why men become anxious. Just as a medical doctor might outline three stages in an illness as it progresses, so Jesus teaches that anxiety is a moral sickness that can be traced to three factors in our lives.

1. *Having your treasure in the wrong place.* By 'treasure,' Jesus means the things we prize most dearly. There are only two places for our treasure to be – in heaven or on earth. Every earth-bound treasure is liable to fail – through deterioration ('moth and rust destroy') or

through unforeseen circumstances ('thieves break in and steal'). Only heaven is immune from the ravages of time and sin. 'Therefore,' says Jesus, 'bank in heaven, not on earth.' Live for heaven, not for earth!

What our Lord says here is devastatingly simple. When he says it, it seems so obvious. If we would only think seriously about our possessions, we would realise that they belong to a passing world, which offers no security. In fact, seeking security in this world and its possessions is a recipe for producing anxieties, rather than relieving them! The more we gather possessions in order to feel secure, the more we feel we need them in order to be secure and then the more we need to guard them to maintain our security. Therefore, the less secure we are! It is a familiar saying that wealth does not buy happiness. Here Jesus explains why. Happiness depends on *lasting* wealth.

This teaching could hardly be more appropriate for the church than it is today. Some parts of the church are almost totally engulfed by teaching that appears on the surface to be 'spiritual,' but simply panders to the anxiety of the worldly heart. It offers health and wealth, happiness and joy as the inevitable accompaniments of faith.

Instead of delivering us from our fascination with this world, such teaching only immerses us further in it. We fall into the error of taking material prosperity as the ultimate mark of God's blessing, whereas Jesus tells us the marks of God's blessing are poverty of spirit, mourning for sin, and persecution for the sake of righteousness. Real spirituality is not seen in the gathering of wealth, but in being delivered from loving it – whether we have it or do not have it.

This is why Jesus' parable of the sower and the soils is so deeply penetrating. The seed is sown among thorns, where it begins to grow. But the thorns grow also, and choke the good seed. What are these thorns? Jesus

[137]

explains that they are 'the worries of this life, the deceitfulness of wealth and the desires for other things' (*Mk. 4:18–19*). When we set our hearts on wealth, for whatever reason, it always deceives us.

In recent years it has become popular to speak of some Christians as 'too heavenly-minded to be of any earthly use.' It is a clever, but incorrect, axiom. Of course there are pious people who, like the Pharisees, separate themselves from the world in which they live, lest they be contaminated by it. These people are known by what they refuse to do, rather than by the grace, love, and joy of Christ that they exhibit. But that kind of piety is not true heavenly-mindedness. It can sometimes be the symptom of a false holiness that serves as the veneer of a heart absorbed with self.

The man or woman who is truly heavenly-minded is the one who brings the atmosphere of heaven down to earth and lives a life of practical holiness. Having treasure in heaven, such a person is delivered from grasping and maintaining his status in this world. He alone is really free to serve others.

Where is your treasure? What in life do you count as really important? What do you dream about? More important, what do you day-dream about? Perhaps that is the clearest index of where your treasure really lies. What *occupies* your mind? Wrong priorities breed anxious hearts.

2. *Thinking about life in the wrong way.* We use different metaphors in English from those that were common in the Aramaic language that Jesus spoke. But his point is not difficult to grasp. The picture Jesus gives is extremely vivid. When our eyes are healthy, our 'whole body is full of light.' If our eyes are diseased, then our 'whole body will be full of darkness' (*6:22–23*). When we see clearly, this world is full of light, colour and beauty. But if our

eyes are diseased, the world is dim, confusing, and even dark as night.

Our Lord is speaking about 'the eye of the spirit,' the heart. In the language of Scripture, fixing the eye and fixing the heart amount to the same thing – focusing our attention and concentrating all our energies on something.

Jesus is saying that the dark spirit of anxiety that grips so many lives is caused by failure to focus spiritually, and by thinking about life with a mistaken – or diseased – perspective. That diseased eyesight affects more than the eyes. The greater tragedy is that 'the whole body is full of darkness.' So it is with our hearts. Poor spiritual vision – having wrong spiritual priorities – influences the entire direction of our lives.

Most of us have had eyesight tests of the most basic kind. A large chart of letters is placed before us. We read down the chart. The letters become smaller and smaller. We reach a point at which we find C difficult to distinguish from O, although we can still distinguish it from Z. But eventually all of the letters become indistinguishable from one another.

When children at school endure such tests, they often ask one another, 'Which line did you reach?' It is a good question for us to ask. The Sermon on the Mount provides us with an admirable test of our spiritual vision as we read through it. Which line of it can you reach? Can you read as far as verse 33? 'Seek first his kingdom and his righteousness, and all these things will be given to you as well. Therefore do not worry about tomorrow.' Or has your vision of that command become clouded, so that it does not seem to you to be quite as vital as it once did?

3. *Serving a master of the wrong kind.* You cannot serve two masters, says Jesus. He is not saying that it is impossible to 'moonlight.' Rather, he is suggesting that the effort to do so leads to tension and anxiety.

[139]

We should notice the obvious implication of Jesus' teaching here. We were made to have a master; God made us for himself. He is Lord, whether we think so or not. We are created in such a way that worship is an integral part of our nature. But when we turn from worshipping the Lord, we do not cease to be worshipping creatures. Instead of being the servants of the Lord, whose service is perfect freedom, we become slaves to what God has made, and even to what man has made – possessions. As Paul points out, we have 'exchanged the truth of God for a lie, and worshiped and served created things rather than the Creator – who is forever praised. Amen' (*Rom. 1:25*).

For the Christian, whose calling it is to be the servant of God, such compromise of loyalties leads to uncertainty, to anxiety, and ultimately to spiritual disaster – now loving one master, now serving another master. It is vital for our spiritual well-being that the question of our devotion be settled once and for all. Have you resolved that issue?

The apostle Paul speaks about this in a particularly searching way. He is concerned that the church at Corinth should be free from any anxiety that would mar their witness and detract from their wholehearted surrender to the Lord's service. He writes:

What I mean, brothers, is that the time is short. From now on those who have wives should live as if they had none; those who mourn, as if they did not; those who are happy, as if they were not; those who buy something, as if it were not theirs to keep; those who use the things of the world, as if not engrossed in them. For this world in its present form is passing away. I would like you to be free from concern.

(1 Cor. 7:29–32)

What does Paul mean? Are we to become 'world-haters,' seeing possessions, marriage, and commerce as hindrances to the Christian life? The kingdom of God has drawn near. As Paul puts it, the time is short and the world in its present form is passing away. Does that fact summon us to live as monks and hermits? Surely not. Paul himself knew how to abound as well as how to be in want (*Phil. 4:12*).

What Paul means (as does Jesus) is that life in the kingdom of God calls for single-minded allegiance to the King. In that context, we are stewards of everything we have – family, home, business. We do not possess them. They are gifts given by the Lord, the blessings of his rule over us. They are never, ever, to become our masters, or even to compete with him for mastery over us. We must not let them do so. If we love them, without first of all remembering that they are his, we will soon hate and despise the one who gave them to us (*Matt. 6:24*).

When you visit your doctor, he asks a series of questions in order to diagnose your condition. When Jesus conducts his diagnosis of our condition, he also has questions: *Where is your treasure? On what is your spiritual vision focused? Who is your Master?* Our answers to these questions tell a great deal about our spiritual well-being.

JESUS' PRESCRIPTION

Anxiety, we have seen, is a symptom of deep spiritual sickness. It is one thing to know that, but another to be able to cure our anxiety. Jesus speaks about curing it: 'I tell you, do not worry' (*6:25*).

In itself, that is an inadequate cure! Imagine being told that you are quite seriously ill. How would you react if your doctor said, 'But don't worry'? You would probably reply, 'Only when you tell me there is a cure for my illness will I be able to stop worrying.'

Diagnosis is insufficient if it does not lead to treatment. That is why Jesus' exhortation, 'Do not worry,' is set in the context of specific teaching that helps to free us from paralysing anxiety about our lives. The teaching in Matthew 6:25–34 is calculated to act as an antidote to worry.

In essence, Jesus says to us, 'Sit down. There are several issues that you need to think through.' *Think through* is the important phrase because healing of the diseased spirit – the process Scripture calls 'sanctification' – begins in the mind. The transformation of our character begins with the renewing of our mind (*Rom. 12:2*). Only when we think with minds that have been instructed by Christ will we begin to live in a way that benefits the kingdom of Christ.

But where shall we find this instruction? Our present activity of studying the Sermon on the Mount answers that question. God transforms our lives by the renewing of our minds as we study and submit to the teaching of Scripture! In it, God's Spirit opens our eyes to understand spiritual things. We gain a right perspective (God's perspective) on the world and our activities in it. Scripture has the very practical purpose of 'teaching, rebuking, correcting and training in righteousness, so that the man of God may be thoroughly equipped for every good work' (*2 Tim. 3:16*).

In this particular section of Scripture, a series of directives is given to us with the intention of renewing our minds so that our lives become consistent with the kingdom in which we live. This is Jesus' antidote for anxiety.

1. *Look at the whole of life.* Have you ever noticed what happens when you become anxious about something? It begins to dominate your thinking, and you see everything in the light of your anxiety. It seems (to you) that everything depends on resolving your anxiety, and, indeed (to you), everything in your life seems related to it.

You get caught in a vicious circle. When your anxiety is about what you eat, or drink, or the clothes you wear, it is not long before your whole life and your happiness seem to depend on these things. These basic servants become your masters.

The Christian is not indifferent to eating, drinking, or clothes. They are necessities for living in this world and in society. But they are never his masters. He has learned that he does not need to eat in the most fashionable restaurants in town or cook the most elegant meals in order to live life to the full. Nor does he need the latest fashion in clothes to feel 'accepted' where it really matters. Jesus has taught him that 'life is more than food and the body more than clothes.'

Open a glossy magazine and read the advertisements. What do so many of them tell you? Life is centred on food, drink, and clothing. One can verify this by glancing through most glossy magazines. Almost without exception, the advertisements proclaim the virtues of food, drink, and dress in one form or another. Some advertisements even announce the brand of cat food that will make your feline friend look her best!

What has happened? The basic necessities of life – life's servants, as it were – have become our masters. But, Jesus says, there is more to life than food. The person whose life is expressed through a body is far more important than the clothes it wears.

How, then, are we to think about these things? Jesus bids us to look at the whole of life. The birds of the air and the flowers of the field demonstrate what an exquisite designer and provider God is. If he provides with a tender, fatherlike care for these, how much more will he provide for the people he has purchased at the infinite cost of the death of his Son (*Rom. 8:32*)? Can you not believe that the Lord will provide for you everything you need in your life?

Do you ever use that argument? You should, frequently – and not with a secretly disgruntled spirit! Your Father knows your needs. He loves you. He will supply all you need.

2. *Look at the nature of life.* 'Who of you by worrying can add a single hour to his life?' asks Jesus (6:27). No one can, obviously. But what is Jesus' point? Is it simply, 'Worrying never got anyone anywhere'? Surely anyone with a little sense could have said that.

Jesus' point is more profound. He has been speaking about his Father's provision for our lives. Now he underlines the nature of the Christian's life: 'Your life is in the hands of your Father. He has designed it. He knows the end of it from the beginning. He plans each step of the way to fulfil his purpose for you and through you. You will have all you need to fulfil that purpose, and when that is accomplished, you will be taken home to be with him. Why worry when he has your life in his hands? Your worry is a sign that you do not adequately know him, or that you do not trust him, or have not yet yielded to him as you ought.'

It is only when we want to take our lives out of the Father's hands and have them under our own control that we find ourselves gripped with anxiety. The secret of freedom from anxiety is freedom from ourselves and abandonment of our own plans. But that spirit emerges in our lives only when our minds are filled with the knowledge that our Father can be trusted implicitly to supply everything we need.

This is why the Bible has so much to say about the sovereign rule of God. In the mists of theological arguments, we often lose sight of that. But the whole of the Sermon on the Mount depends on the fact that God rules this world, that his ways are perfect, and that his purposes will be brought to pass. Our petitions that his will be done on earth as in heaven, and that his kingdom come, claim his promise that thus it will be one day. They express our personal commitment to whatever his will for our lives might be. Only those who appreciate this can say of themselves, 'Our lives are immortal until our work for God is done.'

It is God, our Father, who sets the boundaries of our lives, who prepares good works in advance, for us to accomplish (*Eph. 2:10*), and who promises that when we live according to his plan, we shall lack nothing. When we see that, then we also see the pointlessness of anxiety, and the purposefulness of trusting everything to him.

3. *Look at the Lord's generosity.* We noticed earlier, in studying Jesus' teaching on hypocrisy, that one element in the make-up of the Pharisee was his sinister suspicion of the Father's grace. Like the elder brother of the prodigal son, the Pharisee thought of himself as 'slaving for God.' That was an echo from the first temptation in the Garden of Eden, when Satan insinuated that God had been miserly, indeed cynical, in the way he had set Adam and Eve in a garden, but had forbidden them from really enjoying themselves (*Gen. 3:1-5*).

The devil succeeded in uprooting Eve from a joyful trust in the Father's lavish provision. But she was not alone in entertaining and acting on doubts about the Father's grace. Men by nature doubt it, for Satan has been successful in persuading them that God's presence in their lives will mar them forever.

Many of our anxieties – and our reluctance to take the divine medicine for them – spring from this basic suspicion. But Jesus demolishes it in Matthew 6:24-30. No Christian who properly appreciates what he is saying should be deceived again.

'Look at how the Father cares for the birds of the air,' says Jesus. 'He provides for them. And you are far more valuable than they are.' This is known technically as an argument *a minore ad maius* ('from the lesser to the greater'). If *X* is true, then how much more true *Y* will be. If the Father cares for little birds, how much more will he care for his people who have been created to show his glory and speak his praises?

Jesus also says, 'Look at the lilies of the field. They have no anxious toil to produce their beauty. But not even Solomon's glorious apparel can compare with theirs.' Isn't that true? Look at the flowers – the delicacy of the colours, the magnificent combinations of hues and shades. We compliment designers who can even approximate the beauty and originality of nature in their 'creations.' 'Well,' says Jesus, 'if God has so lavishly provided for these creatures of a season, "here today and tomorrow thrown into the fire" [*6:30*], how much more will he provide for your needs!'

The logic is irrefutable. Let it grip your mind, and you will be free from pursuing what the faithless pagans seek (*6:32*). Notice Jesus' language here. He says that the pagans 'run after all these things.' They know nothing else worth pursuing. But the Christian 'runs after' the Lord (*Ps. 42:1*)! How foolish to seek the gift when it is possible to seek the Giver.

4. *Seek first the kingdom of God.* Anxiety can never be cured by getting more of what we have already. Many people make that fatal mistake. Anxiety can be cured only by the assurance that all our needs will be met by our King. For this reason, the chief drive in our lives should be to live under the authority of the king and to see his kingdom extended in every possible way – morally, socially, and geographically, as well as personally, inwardly, and spiritually. When our hearts are set on his righteousness pervading our lives, we have our priorities in order, and will discover two things:

First, all we need, he will provide. He has never failed one of his children.

Second, many of the things we thought we needed we now discover we did not really need, and do not now want. At last, in place of anxiety, we have found contentment.

We live in days of great anxiety and uncertainty. The very foundations of life sometimes seem to be on the verge of collapse. No wonder we are anxious. But why should we be, when God, who rules all things, has become *our Father*? It is not rational or reasonable to be anxious when he has promised to supply all our needs.

If, in the face of Jesus' teaching, we remain anxious, it is either because we do not yet understand him, or we do not yet trust him. In either case, the fault is ours, not his. For he not only diagnoses the cause of worry; he provides its cure. He *is* its cure.

Are you being cured yet?

13
20/20 Vision

MATTHEW 7

'Do not judge, or you too will be judged. ²For in the same way you judge others, you will be judged, and with the measure you use, it will be measured to you.

³'Why do you look at the speck of sawdust in your brother's eye and pay no attention to the plank in your own eye? ⁴How can you say to your brother, "Let me take the speck out of your eye," when all the time there is a plank in your own eye? ⁵You hypocrite, first take the plank out of your own eye, and then you will see clearly to remove the speck from your brother's eye.

⁶'Do not give dogs what is sacred; do not throw your pearls to pigs. If you do, they may trample them under their feet, and then turn and tear you to pieces.

⁷'Ask and it will be given to you; seek and you will find; knock and the door will be opened to you. ⁸For everyone who asks receives; he who seeks finds; and to him who knocks, the door will be opened.

⁹'Which of you, if his son asks for bread, will give him a stone? ¹⁰Or if he asks for a fish, will give him a snake? ¹¹If you, then, though you are evil, know how to give good gifts to

*your children, how much more will your Father in heaven give
good gifts to those who ask him!* ¹²*In everything, do to others
what you would have them do to you, for this sums up the Law
and the Prophets.'*

★   ★   ★

The Sermon on the Mount, as we have seen, has a
wonderfully unified theme. We would expect that from
the master preacher and teacher of the church. It would,
therefore, be wrong to try to find artificial divisions in its
structure. But there is *development* in different ways, as
the sermon leads on to its conclusion and climax.

The chapter divisions in our Bibles (which were not, of
course, in the original manuscripts) mark one element in
this development. Generally speaking, we can say that
chapter five emphasises the coming of the kingdom of God
and its implications, especially in relation to the law of
God. Chapter six emphasises the Fatherhood of God and
the freedom the knowledge of it gives us. Chapter seven
emphasises the judgment of God, and the impact this
makes on the way we live.

For many people, Christians included, the very mention of the judgment of God brings a sense of dis-ease.
They find it difficult to think of God both as Father and
Judge. Surely (they imagine) he must be either/or. But no
one who has been instructed in Scripture and is sensitive
to its teaching should fall into that false dichotomy.
Certainly anyone whose reading of Scripture has brought
him into the very presence of God himself could never
doubt that these two aspects of God's character go
hand-in-hand.

God is *both* Father and Judge. The terrible thing for the
unbeliever is that he *is* both; in rejecting God's judgment
on his life, the unbeliever also rejects the privilege of

having him as his Father; in rejecting God's fatherly grace, the unbeliever encounters him as Judge. For the believer, the knowledge that God is Father transforms his view of him as Judge, and the knowledge that he is Judge fills him with awe that such a God is also his Father.

Admittedly, however, it often easier for us to sense the wonder of these two aspects of God's character than it is for us coherently to describe them. We cannot reduce them to a lower common denominator. We have to think about both, usually one after the other. So, as the master teacher, Jesus first expounds what it means to have God as our Father, then what it means to recognise him as our Judge.

Knowing God as Judge has a sanctifying and restraining influence on our lives. In particular, it has the effect of making us pursue holiness of heart and life more rigorously. God's position as Judge teaches us to be stricter with ourselves in the sense of dealing with our sin with a persistent determination to master it.

But at the same time, an awareness of God as Judge teaches us to be merciful, and gentle with others. For in the discovery of our own hearts, we learn to have compassion on others in their weakness. The knowledge of God's judgment clarifies and sanctifies our attitudes toward ourselves and others, as well as toward the Lord. In Matthew 7:1–11 we find these three dimensions developed in detail.

SEEING MORE CLEARLY

'Do not judge, or you too will be judged,' says Jesus (7:1). His reason follows: the measure of judgment God uses for us will be the measure we have used in our own judgment of others. That does not mean that God will use the same vindictive principle we sometimes use. Rather,

Jesus is saying that the judgment of God on our lives will be based *on our lives*, and how our hearts expressed themselves in thoughts and acts towards others. So, Jesus warns us, 'Judge not.'

These words may be among the most misunderstood teaching in the Sermon on the Mount. Frequently we hear them cited when, for example, someone comments on a situation and condemns evil. 'Judge not,' someone else will say, seeming to imply, 'Don't ever say something is wrong. It isn't up to you to judge.'

The logical conclusion of such an attitude would be to treat good and evil alike and regard moral distinctions as matters of indifference. But that would fly in the face of the rest of the Bible, especially Jesus' teaching in this section of the sermon. In verse 6, he specifically encourages us to make judgments: 'Do not give dogs what is sacred; do not throw your pearls to pigs.' Jesus is talking about men and women. Spiritually, some people behave like dogs and pigs, he says. We need to recognise them and deal with them appropriately. That calls for a certain kind of judgment to be made.

What, then, does Jesus mean? The answer lies in the illustration he uses. It is one of the most vivid in the sermon, and surely brought smiles to the faces of his hearers. At the same time, it probably scratched where some of them itched!

'Do you see that man?' asks Jesus. 'He has a plank of wood in his eye! But what on earth is he doing? Listen to him! "My friend," the man is saying, "I see there is a tiny speck of dust in the corner of your eye. Let me get it out for you." Isn't that ridiculous?'

What is wrong with such a man? He is looking for sins in other people, and he pounces whenever he sees one. So absorbed is he in his campaign that he is blind to the fact that he has sin in his own life that is far greater than anything he sees in the lives of others. In fact, his pursuit of others' sins (which he regards as proof of his good standing with God) is like a plank of wood compared to a speck of sawdust. He is guilty of the sin of *censoriousness*. So deeply has his sin conquered him that he has become blind to it. Sensitive to sin in others, he has been desensitised to the sin in his own heart.

That spirit often begins as a defence mechanism. We are sensitive to our own failure, but when challenged about it, we pounce on the sins of others. Soon that guilty sensitivity becomes a habit, and then a way of life.

This, says Jesus, is the ultimate tragedy of the hypocrite. He reaches the place where he is acting a part in order to hide from others and from himself the real nature of his own sin and guilt. But now he has confused acting with reality. He is deluded into thinking that he has become what he once knew he could only pretend to be – better than others. Instead of softening his heart, his earlier discovery of his sinfulness has only hardened it.

This spirit of censoriousness has a common symptom. It often manifests itself by flying into a rage against some injustice. Do not misunderstand. It is right to be opposed to each injustice we encounter. But sudden and strong outbursts of emotion can sometimes be signs of a sensitivity that is personal rather than moral and spiritual.

David's life furnishes an obvious illustration of a hardened heart. He sinned seriously because of his lust for Bathsheba. He committed adultery with her and arranged for the death of her husband (*2 Sam. 11:1–17*). But the Lord sent the prophet Nathan to tear the scales from David's eyes. Like our Lord, Nathan used a parable, although at first David did not realise it. Notice what Nathan said, but especially notice David's response:

The Lord sent Nathan to David. When he came to him, he said, 'There were two men in a certain town, one rich and the other poor. The rich man had a very large number of sheep and cattle, but the poor man had nothing except one little ewe lamb he had bought. He raised it, and it grew up with him and his children. It shared his food, drank from his cup and even slept in his arms. It was like a daughter to him.

'Now a traveller came to the rich man, but the rich man refrained from taking one of his own sheep or cattle to prepare a meal for the traveller who had come to him. Instead, he took the ewe lamb that belonged to the poor man and prepared it for the one who had come to him.'

David burned with anger against the man and said to Nathan, 'As surely as the Lord lives, the man who did this deserves to die! He must pay for that lamb four times over, because he did such a thing and had no pity.'

Then Nathan said to David, 'You are the man!'

(2 Sam. 12:1–7)

I am not for a moment suggesting that any man who burns with anger against unrighteousness is a hypocrite. God alone knows the heart of each man. But what is clear in David's case, and implied in Jesus' teaching, is that to have strong feelings about the sins of others that are not matched by a ruthless dealing with our own sins is *hypocrisy*. And further, outbursts of anger can be the expressions of a heart that does not know how to say, 'There, but for the grace of God, go I.'

The heart that has tasted the Lord's grace and forgiveness will always be restrained in its judgment of others. It has seen itself deserving judgment and condemnation before the Lord, and yet, instead of experiencing his burning anger, has tasted his infinite mercy.

This, incidentally, further explains our Lord's woes against the Pharisees (*Matt. 23*). They made God to be like themselves. They had never tasted his grace, and so they did not know that he was gracious to sinners. That is the

[153]

tragedy of the hypocrite (*7:5*). He needs to stand under God's judgment of his life, and then he will be able to see clearly to deal sensitively with the sins and failures of others.

SEEING OTHERS MORE CLEARLY

'Do not judge,' Jesus says. 'But, on the other hand, do not be insensitively undiscriminating.' This is the meaning of the isolated statement he makes in verse 6: 'Do not give dogs what is sacred; do not throw your pearls to pigs. If you do, they may trample them under their feet, and then turn and tear you to pieces.' These words have several levels of application.

They certainly apply to the disciples' work in evangelism. The whole world is to be the sphere of the church's outreach (*Matt. 28:18–20*). There is to be universal preaching of the kingdom of God. Men and women everywhere must be urged to repent and believe the gospel. But that is not a command to engage mindlessly in evangelism. There are those who obviously and stubbornly reject the gospel. They trample the pearls of the message like pigs, Jesus says, and may then do the same to you. You must be sensitive to that kind of response, and recognise the indications that the time has come to offer the gospel to others elsewhere.

This discernment was present in the ministry of Jesus and the apostles. When Jesus sent them to the 'lost sheep of Israel,' he counselled them that whenever their message was rejected they should shake the dust off their feet as they left that home or town (*Matt. 10:14*). Later, in the evangelism of the early church, a similar pattern developed. When the gospel was rejected, the apostles moved on. (There are examples of this in *Acts 13:44–46*, *18:5–6*, and *28:23–31*). Jesus did not entrust himself to some men (*Jn. 2:24*) because that would be to cast his pearls before swine. We need to learn spiritual discernment from him.

How do we recognise those whom Jesus thus describes? By their response to the gospel. They do not appreciate its worth; they treat it as commonplace. As far as they can see, there is no difference between the pearls that are spread before them in the message of God's grace, and what they have always been used to. They see nothing special about the gospel. If you press them further, you will discover their deep hostility to it erupting in opposition and even persecution.

One of the lessons we need to learn, therefore, is to live with the cost of our message being rejected. While that is heartbreaking, we are taught in Scripture that it will happen. Forewarned is forearmed. We are not taken by surprise by rejecters of the gospel. We do not mindlessly continue to offer Christ to people irrespective of their response.

Again, we see this in the witness of the early church. In response to the gospel, people cried out, 'Brothers, what shall we do?' because they were cut to the heart (*Acts 2:37*). When asked, 'What must I do to be saved?' (*Acts 16:30*), the early Christians patiently explained the gospel and urged those who heard to respond in repentance and faith. But if the message of Christ was rejected, they did not outstay their welcome (for example, *Acts 13:46*).

There is a more general principle underlying the words in verse 6: *the wisdom of appropriate activity*. Why do we not cast pearls before swine? Because it is inappropriate to do so. The person who does so does not understand either the value of pearls or the nature of pigs! Yet, how often we find Christians engaged in activities, or behaving in a fashion altogether inappropriate for the gospel or for their position as believers. It may well be that Jesus is thinking here of this more general application. Perhaps he was making good use of a Palestinian proverb.

Sometimes we Christians are not very wise, as Jesus seems to have realised (see *Lk. 16:8*). On occasion we get stuck in the rut of a tradition that it is not in itself biblical. We fail to recognise that the words we use or the precise activities in which we engage are *no longer appropriate*. Instead of showing the contemporary relevance of the gospel, we veil that relevance and strip it of its power.

By our actions, we are really conveying an unspoken message that the gospel belongs to a past generation, or is permanently enshrined in some ancient tradition. But Christ and the gospel are always contemporary. We need to see to it that we live, speak, act, and witness in ways that are appropriate to him and to our times.

SEEING GOD MORE CLEARLY

In verses 7–12, the theme of Jesus' preaching seems to change rather abruptly as he begins to speak of asking, seeking and knocking. Bible commentators have sometimes remarked that the connecting link between this passage and what preceded it is not at all clear. Why turn from the themes of judgment and discernment to that of prayer?

It may be that verses 7–12 deal with something more broadly based than prayer – namely, the need the children have for their Father's provision, counsel, and direction and their consequent obligation to show the Father's love in their dealings with others.

No one can follow the sermon up to this point without becoming profoundly aware of his need. We are beggars before God. We are spiritually shortsighted and undiscerning. We fall so far short of what we should be for the sake of our Lord Jesus. We have nothing to offer him.

Here, then, Jesus teaches us what has rightly been called 'beggars' logic.' We are to persist in asking for God's grace as though we are beggars (for spiritually, we always remain so). We can do so in the confidence that the one who responds to our asking, who reveals himself to our seeking, and who opens his heart to our knocking, is a Father to us!

Jesus presses this point home with an argument similar in format to one he used earlier in the sermon (*6:26*). If earthly fathers, sinful as they are, give good gifts to their children, *how much more* will the heavenly Father give good gifts to his children when they ask him?

But why does Jesus return to his stress on the fatherhood of God here? Because, as we have already noticed, his concern is that we should discover that our Judge is our Father. The truth about God, and therefore true knowledge of God, does not lie in one or the other of these characteristics, but in both. We shall never really understand the wonder of his grace until, seeking mercy like beggars before a judge, we discover that he wants us to be his sons and daughters.

It certainly is a wonderful thing that God justifies sinners, and that, as the righteous Judge of all the earth, he is able to acquit us. But Jesus points to something that seems to belong to a higher order of things. This Judge takes out adoption papers on our behalf, places his hands on our shoulders and says, 'My child, I want you to share in the inheritance of all my riches and blessings. You will be my son, my daughter, from now on. Come with me, and ask me when you are in need.'

This explains why Jesus concludes this section of the sermon with a statement that otherwise seems quite out of place: 'In everything, do to others what you would have them do to you, for this sums up the Law and the Prophets.' What at first sounds like an isolated statement, quite unrelated to what precedes it, is actually intimately related. Only the person who sees that he is a beggar before the Lord and has nothing to offer – but has discovered that he is heir of the grace of God – will be sufficiently set free from self-centredness of character to put others first, and to do to them what he would appreciate receiving from them.

We see, then, that living under the judgement of God is not a cause for cringing fear, as Satan suggests. It is the remedy for self-absorption and the way to genuine spiritual freedom, in which we serve the Lord and are happy to serve others, too.

Do you 'do to others what you would have them do to you'? It is a limitless exhortation. When this 'golden rule' has appeared in the teaching of others (from Confucius to Immanuel Kant), it has usually been stated in the negative: 'Do not do to others what you do not want them to do to you.' In that form, it is always less demanding. It forbids action. It does not prescribe it. It sets limits. But what *Jesus* says is limitless in its demands and scope. His teaching is both positive and all-embracing in our lives.

But Jesus' statement is also simplifying. Here he gives us a summary of the law and the prophets. He does not mean that because we know this text, we can ignore all others. Rather, he is suggesting that this counsel gives us in a nutshell the principle that is expounded and illustrated in a thousand and more ways in the rest of Scripture ('the law and the prophets' being representative of the whole Old Testament).

For Jesus, the word of God is not an impossible complex of rules and regulations placed on men's shoulders as a heavy burden. Rather, it is the outworking of this principle of love. Grasp this, and everything falls into place. That is his point.

The Christian life is indeed demanding, but in essence,

its principle is simple. It is knowing the grace of God working so powerfully in your heart that you are freed from the mastery of sin and self over your life. You can now serve others and bring blessing to them as the Lord has brought blessing to you. This is the kind of clear-sightedness that arises from living in the light of the judgement of God your Father.

> *I ask Thee for a thoughtful love,*
> *Through constant watching wise,*
> *To meet the glad with joyful smiles,*
> *And to wipe the weeping eyes,*
> And a heart at leisure from itself,
> To soothe and sympathise.

Anna Laetitia Waring

14
Choices

MATTHEW 7

[13]*'Enter through the narrow gate. For wide is the gate and broad is the road that leads to destruction, and many enter through it.* [14]*But small is the gate and narrow the road that leads to life, and only a few find it.*

[15]*'Watch out for false prophets. They come to you in sheep's clothing, but inwardly they are ferocious wolves.* [16]*By their fruit you will recognise them. Do people pick grapes from thornbushes, or figs from thistles?* [17]*Likewise every good tree bears good fruit, but a bad tree bears bad fruit.* [18]*A good tree cannot bear bad fruit, and a bad tree cannot bear good fruit.* [19]*Every tree that does not bear good fruit is cut down and thrown into the fire.* [20]*Thus, by their fruit you will recognise them.*

[21]*'Not everyone who says to me, "Lord, Lord," will enter the kingdom of heaven, but only he who does the will of my Father who is in heaven.* [22]*Many will say to me on that day, "Lord, Lord, did we not prophesy in your name, and in your name drive out demons and perform many miracles?"* [23]*Then I will tell them plainly, "I never knew you. Away from me, you evildoers!"'*

²⁴'*Therefore everyone who hears these words of mine and puts them into practice is like a wise man who built his house on the rock.*²⁵*The rain came down, the streams rose, and the winds blew and beat against that house; yet it did not fall, because it had its foundation on the rock.*²⁶*But everyone who hears these words of mine and does not put them into practice is like a foolish man who built his house on sand.*²⁷*The rain came down, the streams rose, and the winds blew and beat against that house, and it fell with a great crash.'*

²⁸*When Jesus had finished saying these things, the crowds were amazed at his teaching,*²⁹*because he taught as one who had authority, and not as their teachers of the law.*

*   *   *

True preaching has several functions. Sometimes we make the mistake of thinking it has only one. But sermons are meant to instruct us, shape and transform our thinking and feeling, and challenge us to a new course of action. We sometimes say they should always call for 'decision.' In a sense that is true. But they should do more: they should let God's word loose, so that by its own power it changes its hearers' lives.

This may be one of the reasons Jesus regularly spent extended periods of time preaching to people. That is one of the neglected lessons of the miracles of his feeding the multitudes. If these crowds had been with him long enough to need to be fed, he must have given them *hours* of teaching (*see Mk. 8:2*). He was not merely playing on their wills, calling them to decision. He was patiently expounding to them the truth of God, believing that the good seed of the word has its own power when planted in fertile hearts.

The Sermon on the Mount illustrates this principle. Of course, everywhere we look in it we find moral challenge. But we also find instruction, illumination, 'teaching,

rebuking, correcting [or healing], and training in righteousness,' as Paul puts it (*2 Tim. 3:16*).

It is on this basis that Jesus leads up to the climax of the
sermon, in which he presents to us the decisions and
choices that his teaching demands. All the way through the
sermon it has been obvious that there are only two ways to
live: the way of the Lord and the way of the world (however
disguised in religious dress that may be). Now, in his
closing words, our Lord challenges us to make up our
minds. There are certain issues that must be settled. There
can be no room for negotiation or compromise. A choice has
to be made.

Matthew 7:13–29 sets before us choices in three different
areas: the choice of *the direction of our lives* – will we choose
the right entrance, and walk on Christ's way? Then there is
the choice of *influences* – to what kind of teaching and
teachers will we submit? Finally, there is the most basic
choice of all – what kind of *foundation* have we been laying?

This section of the sermon is about choices. If we were to
give it a sub-title, we might use an expression of C. S. Lewis,
'Undeceptions.' In keeping with the rest of the sermon,
Jesus is vigorously underlining the difference between
what things may seem to be and what they are in reality.
There is always a certain appeal in the broad way, in the
false teacher, in the immediate success story. But we need
to be warned by Jesus that the principles on which the
kingdom of God is established are very different.

THE CHOICE OF ENTRANCES

The illustration of two ways for men to go is used regularly
in Scripture (*Prov. 15:19; Ps. 1:1–6; Jer. 21:8*). Jesus
develops it in some detail in a series of contrasts:

The choice of entrance: Will we go through the wide gate,
or the small gate?

The choice of roads: Will we walk on the way that is broad, or the way that is narrow?

The choice of companions: Will we go with the crowd, or are we prepared to join the few?

The choice of destinies: Will we choose life, or death?

Basically, there is but one choice to be made, between two possible alternatives. Jesus spells out in some detail the implications of those alternatives. Only when we take these implications into account do we realise that the issues before us have a bearing on the whole of our lives – and also on the whole of eternity. 'Do not be deceived,' Jesus is saying, 'what I am setting before you is a life-and-death issue. Look along with me through the gate, right to the final destination. Look at where these entrances will lead you.' He unmasks false appearances.

Many people go through the wide gate and walk along the broad road. They do so for different reasons. Some deliberately reject the way of Christ and choose to abandon his moral demands. Others simply drift along with the crowd, assuming that there is security in numbers. 'After all,' they reason, 'if so-and-so does it, it cannot really be so very harmful.' If only these travellers of the broad road would look right to the end of their pathway, and see that it leads to destruction!

Jesus is urging us, as we make the vital decisions of life, to think things through to their inevitable conclusion in the light of biblical teaching. Only then will we be 'undeceived.'

Christians should never assume that this choice is an easy and obvious one. Sometimes we make that mistake, and by doing so distance ourselves from the real experience and temptations of the people of God in Scripture. They recognised that the wicked often prosper while the Lord's people often suffer. How could they go on choosing the narrow road in the light of this recognition?

Asaph wrestled with that irony in Psalm 73 – one of the most instructive of all the psalms. He saw that those on the broad road prospered. They were often healthier and wealthier than the people of God. In his initial reaction he exclaimed, 'Surely in vain have I kept my heart pure; in vain have I washed my hands in innocence' (*Ps. 73:13*).

Was Asaph unique in his response? Have you never found that frustration coming to the surface in your own life? You struggle, while for others – who are not Christians – life seems to be relatively smooth sailing.

Listen further to Asaph: 'When I tried to understand all this, it was oppressive to me till I entered the sanctuary of God.' Now, why should that action have made a difference? He explains: *'Then I understood their final destiny.'* He saw that the end of the ungodly was ruin. By contrast, he was able to say about his own destiny in God's hands: 'You guide me with your counsel, and afterward you will take me into glory' (*Ps. 73:16-17,24*). In the temple (where he, like Isaiah, found himself in the presence of God's eternal majesty and glory), he saw his own life, and others' lives too, in the light of ultimate reality and God's final judgement. Then he saw who was really being deceived.

This deception is why the New Testament has so much to say about man's future destiny. It does not teach merely 'pie in the sky when you die.' *The very opposite is the case.* It is only when we live in the light of the future, says Jesus, that we can make the right choices *now*. For *appearances* – in any light other than the light of eternity – are bound to deceive.

Have you settled your heart on eternal life? Have you found it in Christ? Then you know not to be influenced by the *ease* of the wide gate and the broad way. You know not to be influenced by *numbers* or *appearances*. If you have been given new life, then you know not to join those who 'follow the ways of this world,' who are following the 'desires and thoughts' of the flesh (*Eph. 2:2–3*).

There is something else you will not be deceived by: the nature of the Christian life. It has a small entrance, since the kingdom of God belongs to those who are 'poor in spirit'. The pathway is narrow, with dangers and temptations along the pilgrim's path. At times there may seem to be very few companions. Sometimes the Christian life can even seem unappealing.

Jesus tells us: *Do not be deceived.* Things are not always what they seem to be. These things may be true, but they are not the whole truth – for the Christian life is filled with blessings. (The kingdom of heaven is ours; we receive the comfort of God; we inherit the earth; we are filled with righteousness; we receive mercy; we see God; we belong to God's family!) Yes, those who leave everything for the sake of Christ and the gospel will experience 'persecutions,' but 'no one who has left home or brothers or sisters or mother or father or children or fields for me and the gospel will fail to receive a hundred times as much in this present age. . . .' (*Mk. 10:29–30*).

B.B.C. television's *Dr Who*, the exiled 'Time Lord', has become a household name in the English-speaking world, as he travels the universe of space and time in his spaceship *The Tardis*. From the outside *The Tardis* looks like an old-fashioned British police box. But on the inside, *The Tardis* is spacious, comfortable, and the setting for a whole world of excitement and adventure.

The paradoxical nature of *The Tardis* bears a striking similarity to what Jesus tells us about the kingdom of God. *Everything depends on whether you experience it from the outside or the inside.* On the inside, we see that the road that at first appeared so narrow is the only one that 'leads to life' (*Matt. 7:14*).

Is this choice settled in your heart?

THE CHOICE OF INFLUENCES

The Christian life is one of spiritual conflict. Those who are recipients of 'every spiritual blessing in Christ Jesus' experience those blessings 'in the heavenly realms' (*Eph. 1:3*). But precisely because we have been brought into those realms, we find ourselves engaged in conflict with 'the spiritual forces of evil *in the heavenly realms*' (*Eph. 6:12*). The sphere of blessing is also the sphere of battle! For no believer ever escapes from Satan without him seeking either to recapture him, or to have vengeance on Christ by hindering his spiritual progress. One of the ways in which he does this is through the influence of 'false prophets' (*Matt. 7:15*). We are to be on the lookout for them. Forewarned is forearmed!

What is a 'false prophet'? We have a tendency to associate prophecy with the foretelling of the future. But in fact that was only a part (and actually a less prominent part) of the prophet's ministry. The basic task of the prophet was to *forth-tell*, not just to *fore-tell*, God's word. He was to explain and apply God's truth to the lives of the people in his own day, as well as speak about the future. Indeed, the reason he was to speak also about the future was to influence the way that his hearers lived in the present. Simply put, a 'prophet' was one who spoke from God. A 'false prophet' is one who falsifies God's word – either by openly contradicting it, or, more likely (as Jesus indicates), by twisting its meaning.

Do you think you could recognise a 'false prophet' right away? Some Christians seem to pride themselves on their ability to do so. But Jesus says that it is not always so easy to do, for they often come 'in sheep's clothing' – looking, even talking, as though they too belonged to the Lord's flock and were followers of the Good Shepherd. False prophets cannot always be recognised immediately. It may take time before their fruit gives away their real nature, and we see that they are actually wolves, not sheep.

Paul explained to the elders of the church at Ephesus one of the reasons why these wolves are so difficult to detect. 'Even from your own number [from among the elders and pastors of the church at Ephesus, which had known Paul's profound biblical teaching over two or three years of ministry] men will arise and distort the truth in order to draw away disciples after them. So be on your guard!' (*Acts 20:30–31*).

How can we recognise these wolves and escape from their harmful influences? Jesus sets before us several important principles.

1. *The false prophet is identified by his attitude toward the people of God*. He is a 'ferocious wolf,' and expresses his true nature by the way he devours the flock. He does not lay down his life for the sheep (as the Good Shepherd did – see John 10:15). Instead, he uses the sheep to serve his own interests. He is not at all like the Lord Jesus.

Diotrephes is an example of such a person (*3 Jn. 9–10*). Instead of guarding the flock of God, and promoting its peace and unity, he destroyed it – and all for the sake of his own reputation.

We should therefore beware of anyone who 'uses' the church. His influence will not lead us nearer to Christ. The true prophet, or shepherd, does not 'lord it over the flock,' but humbly serves it and sets an example for it (*1 Pet. 5:3*).

2. *The false prophet is identified by the fruit of his teaching*. Good trees bear good fruit; bad trees bear bad fruit (*Matt. 7:18*). Faithful men and false men reveal their true identity in two ways: in their own character and in the fruit of their teaching in the character of others. Are they Christlike? Do those who come under their influence

increasingly share those Christlike qualities? Those are the distinguishing marks.

Sometimes the fruit of a 'pseudo-prophet' appears in sinister ways in the lives of his disciples. It often manifests itself in an exclusivism that is unlike the open-heartedness of Christ. When we are unable to benefit from the ministry or teaching of anyone but some single teacher or select group of teachers – and when that spirit is encouraged by them – we are not far from this bad fruit of false teaching. When this exclusivist spirit manifests itself in downgrading or cynically discussing others who have been faithful to the Lord (whatever their gifts or inadequacies), then evil fruit has begun to appear (*cf. 3 Jn. 9–10*). We ought to stop and ask what kind of influence we have allowed to master us.

This influence of false teaching was pervasive in the church at Corinth. Some people obviously preferred the ministry of Peter, or Paul, or the eloquent Apollos. The situation was ripe for the false apostles and prophets who would soon dominate the church. Soon Paul, Peter, and Apollos would all be spoken of with cynical contempt. Attention would be drawn to their present weaknesses or to their past history – Paul was neither attractive nor eloquent; Peter had denied his Lord; Apollos had once been so shaky theologically that he had needed a woman to instruct him (*Acts 18:24–6*)! The cynical undertones are not difficult to imagine.

Such fruit springs from a rotten tree. That tree needs to be cut down.

3. *The false prophet is identified by his priorities*. On the last day, these prophets will say to Jesus, 'Did we not prophesy in your name, . . . and drive out demons and perform many miracles?' But Jesus will reject their claims to him (*Matt. 7:22–23*). Why? They placed success before obedience (only those who do the will of the Father belong

to the kingdom – verse 21). They put their own position before their service. Most obviously, they substituted *gifts* for *grace*.

For all their mysteriousness, Jesus' words teach us a basic lesson in spiritual discernment: it is possible to exercise 'spiritual gifts' (prophecy, miracles, exorcism of demons are specifically mentioned in verse 22), yet be a total stranger to God's saving grace. The astounding things men can do in public is no certain indication of where they stand in private before the judgment of Jesus Christ. What really counts is how we are related to Christ himself. That is why the gospel has so much more to say about the power of Christ changing our characters than about the power of Christ changing the course of nature.

That distinction is a timely warning to our own generation. We are as easily mesmerised by people with unusual powers as was our Lord's generation. We are fascinated by 'signs.' But Jesus is not a wonder-worker; he is a Saviour. He delivers us from sin and transforms us morally to be like himself. That is the fruit of the true prophet of God. The true prophet is far more interested in grace than in gifts – both in his own life and in the lives of those to whom he ministers.

You have chosen the gate through which you will go. But have you continued to expose your life to the influences that will keep you on the way of Christ? Or have you been sidetracked by false teaching and teachers, failing to recognise the sour and harmful fruit they will produce in your life? 'Watch out for false prophets,' says Jesus.

THE CHOICE OF FOUNDATIONS

The Sermon on the Mount concludes with one of Jesus' most vivid illustrations. In essence he tell us: there are two

[169]

ways to respond. One is to put his sermon into practice in obedience; the other is to ignore it. The first response is the path of the wise man; the second is the response of the fool:

'Look at this man building his house. He digs down and down until he finds rock. He lays solid foundations, and then he begins to assemble the superstructure. But his neighbour seems altogether more enterprising. "Who needs foundations?" he asks, and while the first man is still digging, he has completed his entire house. He has made his neighbour look foolish!

'But look again,' says Jesus. 'Both houses are now finished. They seem similar enough, and stable enough too. But watch! The rain comes; there are floods; a wind begins to howl . . . and *crash!* Down goes the house that was built on the sand. *Which man was the real fool, do you think?*'

What does it mean to build on a solid foundation? It means more than hearing God's word taught and becoming familiar with it, or even agreeing with it. We can do all that and still be a spiritual fool (*v. 26*). *Obedience* to Christ's word distinguishes the wise man from his foolish neighbour. Just as the difference between the false and the true prophet is that the true prophet 'does the will of my Father who is in heaven' (*v. 21*), so the difference between the false and the true Christian is that the true Christian puts into practice what he has heard from the Master in this sermon. The point of having choices set before us is that we might *choose*.

Matthew tells us how the people responded to Jesus' teaching. They were amazed by it, and were especially impressed by his authority. He knew what he was speaking about. He had not learned it from traditions and books. He had learned it from *the* Book, and from a living experience of God and men.

We sometimes admire the response of those who listened in amazement to Jesus' sermon – and there is something admirable about it. But there is also something inadequate about it: Matthew pointedly refrains from telling us that the people *obeyed* it. They thought it was the most admirable sermon they had ever heard. Indeed, it is the most admirable sermon *anyone* has ever heard. In fact it is the most admired sermon in human history.

But Jesus did not preach it in order to be admired for his homiletical skills. He preached it to produce obedience. He preached it so that the authority people *recognised* in his preaching might be *realised* in their lives.

You have seen the authority in his sermon. Now, will you submit to it?

> *'Not everyone who says to me,*
> *"Lord, Lord," will enter into the*
> *kingdom of heaven, but only he*
> *who does the will of my Father.'*